Never Give Up!

Lessons the Lord Taught Me
When I Wanted to Quit!

Mike Allard

Victor Numquam Usque!

Never Give Up!

For Mom

Bobbie Jean Bryant
1929-2015

Victor Numquam Usque!

What You'll Find...

Victor Numquam Usque!

From a Friend...

I met Mike Allard more than 30 years ago when we were serving in youth ministry and working on staff at different churches. Mike excelled in everything – he went on to become the Director of Youth Ministry for the South Texas District of the Assemblies of God. Everything Mike touched shined. With him as the District Youth Director, the district youth ministry reached new heights and Mike Allard was da man!

Through the years I joined the chorus of people that sang the praises of Mike Allard. Admittedly, I too am included in one of those who said – I'd like to be like Mike... it seems success just flows out of him effortlessly! On the surface Mike seemed to soar easily – his humor came as a dose of much-needed relief to those of us facing struggles.

Later, my friendship with Mike deepened as he became a Lead Pastor. I am thankful that Mike shares his story and journey through this book, Never Give Up! With amazing honesty and genuine openness, Mike uncovers his heartbreaks, his profound disappointments, and his tearful breaking points. Mike's disarming humor and successes were forged on the anvil of pain. Mike wants everyone who reads this book to experience hope that God steps in when we can't go on.

The story of Mike's journey through dark and crushing moments reminds us that breakdowns are the breeding ground of breakthroughs. In his book, Mike shares scripture and personal experiences of God-ordained, just-in-the-nick-of-time moments of matchless grace.

God's grace comes to those who suffer.

The Mike Allard I and so many envied in early years as the ideal epitome of success without suffering – that person doesn't exist. In fact, his tears and heartaches outnumber those of many of us. What then is the secret to his successes? In his own words **-** **"Victor Numquam Usque!"** Translated it means **"A winner never gives up!"**

Mike, thanks for sharing your story!

Jim D. Rion,
Lead Pastor of Westover Hills Assembly of God,
San Antonio, Texas

Opening Thoughts...

"I quit" is such a shameful declaration. It's the final gurgle. It's the last gasp of air. Your fingers are tired and you just can't hold on any longer. Someone or something is pushing you down further and further. Life is gradually leaving. You feel the end is near. Your eyes are dilated and the last rays of light are being seen. You're begging to live but it would be easier to quit. To give up and give in. You've already thought about it but now you're saying it every day. "I quit. I'm done. I can't go on." It's like you can see the closing credits of your life and you want it all to be over. The end.

Where do you go when you want to quit? Who do you tell? Where do you hide? Where do you run when others have quit on you? When you've quit on yourself? Your thoughts race on endlessly about the future. Your life seems to flash before you. Who will ever listen to a failure? You picture yourself walking out. What will my friends say? How do I tell my family? Your mind tries to imagine the look on the faces of friends and family as you say those final words, "I quit!"

How do you go on? How do you pick up the pieces? Life feels like a garbage bag full of broken promises and you are at the bottom. Nothing seems to ease the pain. Who do you turn to? Where do you run? Where do you hide?

You ask yourself, "Will I ever live again? Will the world ever be normal again? What is normal? Does anyone really care?" These are just a few of the countless questions you ask yourself.

Let me say, "Keep breathing." Keep fighting to get up and go on.

I too faced such a time in my life and it's my desire to bring hope to your journey and share some of what I learned to give you a little encouragement to lean on.

The financial crisis of 2008-2009 was such a season for me. Many families and businesses were ruined during that economic downturn. It's been called the Great Recession.

For me, it was the worst public failure of my life. The shame and humiliation were incomprehensible. It changed my life. It changed my ministry. I was on the anvil of faith. The heavy hammer of reality was crushing me. Every blow was killing what little life I had left.

The following pages are a few of the lessons I learned during my dark season.

Let's walk down that path together. It's rocky and I may stumble over a few of the memories but hopefully you'll hear the story and draw hope from its conclusion. I made it. I survived. And you will too.

A good friend of mine always says, "God's got this!" I believe that. Maybe there's a thread of hope in my story for you. Hang on. Don't quit.

Around my study and in boxes I've kept years of thank you notes: cards, letters, and even Post-Its that people have given me saying: *I appreciate the work you've done. You're awesome. Thank you. Wow, great job! You're amazing. Thank you for your leadership. Keep up the wonderful work.*

It never seemed right to throw away such thoughtful gifts. Their words to me, their well wishes and thoughts of how they felt about me, were precious and were like little paper treasures.

So the antitype of success is failure. For me failure was not a familiar term. Most of what I had been involved in, up to that point, had thrived. This would be a different kind of journey. How would I handle it? How will you handle it? I didn't handle it well. I had days where I lashed out. I had moments of remorse and regret. Overwhelming regret! Nothing I had ever experienced seemed to prepare me for this.

When the big F of failure is all you see every day, you seem to see nothing else. Your trial has come to stay and it looks like it will never leave.

For me, it was the greatest trial of my life. All was gone and there really was nothing worth living for, or so I felt. It was then when I wanted to quit and run. I know you want to run. You want to pack it all up and head out the door. You want to check out and never come back. Not yet. Don't leave. Stay connected. It's during this time you will find the real you. It's the metal of character that's going to come through the fire. The divorce, the failure, the moral collapse, the financial meltdown, or whatever it is that's propelling you to quit is only going to make you stronger.

It was during those days I found the man I would become! It's during this season you will find the person you will become. You will make it.

You are in the biggest trial of your life and you don't know what you'll do. You might be that leader that's lost your way. You're facing a difficult decision with a spouse or child or perhaps you're a pastor like me. You're in a job and you're done. You're sick of the grind and you just want it all to stop.

Perhaps your business is not growing and you're tired and you feel you can't face another day. Maybe you're a pastor and you feel your church is through with you. They are ready for you to leave! Or your family is falling apart and you are the only one willing to stay? Maybe you're in a building program and you hate every day and wonder "how did I get myself into this mess?" Or you have a child or children not serving God; or your spouse has left you. It hurts so bad you want to die. Whatever the case may be, let me encourage you today. Don't give up. Don't quit. Don't surrender.

It's time like this when it seems dying would be easier. You're in such a deep cavern that no voice, no word, no message, nothing can reach your ears. You have shut yourself in and you're in lockdown and your body is going through the motions. You have given up. Life stinks and you want out. You have even contemplated running away and leaving it all - but the Holy Spirit will not let you. You have screamed, "make it all stop!" and it won't. What do you do? What can you do? Who can you trust? Hopefully this does not sound like trivial rehash. Read on - this book is about my journey. I'm sure my journey can't compare to what you're facing, but I wanted to die. I wanted to quit! I threw in the towel. Perhaps there is a pebble of hope you can pick up along my path and skip it across the pond. Hear me, "Don't quit! You're going to make it!"

Chapter 1
He Never Gives Up!

"You can't catch me! You can't catch me!" Dad said, laughing as he ran.

I was only four but I remember it like it was yesterday. Times were simple. Life consisted of playtime and church. My greatest hero was my Dad.

I loved playing this special game with Dad. It was a game of chase. He would lead off and get ahead of me and challenge me to catch him. Chasing him to the church was the best. Being with him was wonderful. I felt loved and cared for. My father was pastor of a little church in San Antonio. As with most pastoral families, church was our life. Serving the Lord was everything. And Dad pretending it was hard for him to get away was special. For me it was so fun and exciting. The thrill of him pulling away and at the last minute allowing me to catch him and the laughter and hugs were the best. Times then were simple and amazing. I miss that. I miss him. I wish I could chase Dad again.

It seems as though we don't cherish the simple things when the simple things are really all there is. The sunset, the night watching TV, the little text messages and the meals where you just sit together... All are so simple but when they're gone, all are so cherished. If only you could get back to that moment again.

We lived in the parsonage connected by a small gravel parking lot just 100 feet away from the church. I have a lot of great memories of my dad preaching and singing the old gospel songs, like "We're Marching to Zion" and "When We All Get to Heaven!" Those were great times, and he was a powerful pastor! I miss that man!

However, we didn't stay in San Antonio for long. When I was almost five, we moved to a little north Texas prairie town called Olney. Dad would pastor another church. It was a beautiful brick-and-stained-glass church that sat on main street. It was the picture of Mayberry and Andy Griffith. The church parsonage sat just behind the dairy mart. I remember a lot of evenings sitting there licking my ice cream cone or root beer float. Life was wonderful.

As a little boy, I remember fiery Pentecostal services, Dad leading the church in Jericho marches, and altar calls that blazed through the night. Growing up, I remember Mom and Dad practicing special songs in the living room of our home. Mom always had a song in her heart! What a faithful servant of the Lord! I love her so much and miss those days hearing her play the organ and lifting her voice in praise. As a little boy, God gave me great parents who imparted to me a huge passion for God.

You Are a Miracle!

Mom often said, "You and your brother are both miracle babies!" Mom and Dad always wanted children, but it was nine years after they married when my brother Jimmy was born. I came along four years later. Both of us were conceived after special prayer at revival services.

That's why Mom always made us feel special. She always gave more than expected and sacrificed everything for her two miracle babies. What a wonderful momma!

Growing Up a Preacher's Kid

I remember occasions when sometimes in the night young couples come by the house, wanting to get married. My brother Jim and I stood in our pajamas, wiping sleep out of our eyes, and witnessed more than one wedding ceremony. That was part of the unforgettable life of a small-town pastor.

When Jim or I would get sick, we didn't take a trip to the doctor. Mom and Dad laid hands on us and used a bottle of anointing oil, and we believed and received our healing time and time again. We were people of faith.

Mom was the church organist and faithfully led the

Women's Missionary Council. I went to Sunday School every Sunday and Vacation Bible School every summer. I never missed a service. We went to church on Sunday morning, Sunday night and Wednesday night. Revivals were usually two weeks long and sometimes longer. That's 14 days straight with no breaks and church every day. Church was everything. One of my favorite toys at church was a tiny plastic Noah's Ark with all the little animals. I will always remember how I loved playing with those toys.

Those were great times. Riding down the highway with the windows down playing airplane with my hand against the wind. Life was simple: playing ball and building forts out of cardboard boxes. It was a beautiful time for our family. Mom and Dad were always there, and what a great team they were. God used them in a mighty way.

It's at this moment that we all remember back and it seems nothing was wrong. Yet behind the scenes there was a lot wrong. Somewhere along the way Dad had lost his way. Communication had broken down between Mom and Dad. Deception had become a daily journey for my father. He was leading us down a dark alley. An alley from which we would leave never the same.

It might be the same for you. You realize that reality is different from the simple life you thought you had. Reality happens to all of us. We all have a reality check of what is really happening.

For us there was a darkness that was growing on the horizon. We would never be the same.

Everything Changed

On September 7, 1967, we moved to Wichita Falls. Dad was no longer pastoring. Sadness filled his life. Hurt and loss was written across my mom's face. Dad's books were packed away and had been moved into the garage. No more ministry and no more revival meetings. We didn't go to church anymore. I was seven, and to me, it all seemed a mystery. I was on the outside looking in. Nothing seemed real. It was like we had traded places with people who weren't us and we were living their lives. It was the opposite of everything I knew before.

In the midst of deep storms sometimes families are ripped apart. Families feel betrayed. Betrayed by friends. Betrayed by organizations. Betrayed by loved ones. Betrayed by one another. It all comes like a massive tidal wave of hurt. You may be a victim in the midst of your storm. Everything was normal up until the time the police knocked on your door or the doctor read the report or you received that phone call. You ask yourself "Why didn't I see it?" Why didn't I do something earlier? If only I had done something differently. You blame yourself.

Being the youngest, I was truly clueless. No one was talking about why we weren't pastoring and as a kid, I guess I just went along. Dad didn't even want to talk about God, church or anything that dealt with that. What had been so common and so much a part of our life was gone.

I remember riding somewhere with Dad during those days and falling asleep in the back seat of our '52 Plymouth. Sometime in the night, I woke up to a strange smell and glowing lights. It was a cigarette. The red glow lit up the car. I had never seen a cigarette in my dad's hands. I froze in fear and dread of what I would see. I closed my eyes and prayed to go to sleep.

I had questions. You have questions. You wonder what you will do? Where will you go? Failure, loss, betrayal, ruin, loneliness, and disaster bring a tsunami of questions.

I wondered what had happened? What was wrong? Why did we have to leave our church? Why did I have to leave my friends, my school? It seemed I had done nothing wrong but I was being punished. Everything that had been normal was gone. Things were good. We were good, but now we were struggling. Joy had left our house. Mom and Dad continued to drift apart.

Dad struggled. He looked for work here and there but

nothing seemed to be a fit. When a man is running from God, nothing is a fit. He was cut out for one thing and he wasn't doing it. He became dark and more distant. He wasn't the man he once was.

Dad

It was somewhere, at that time, that I remember Dad had a pretty bad temper. At times he would get so mad. I was young and thought it was just a part of life. It wouldn't be until later in my life that I could look back and see what was really wrong. I would recall countless times he had acted out in hate the most terrible acts of violence. We were victims and he was destroying our lives.

At an early age Dad had earned his pilot's license. He had a paper route, and earned and saved enough money to eventually take flying lessons. As a result of that love for flying, he had crop dusted on the side while pastoring. Many pastors supplement their incomes with outside work and this was another passion. When I later went into the ministry I supplemented my income with odd jobs.

For Dad, perhaps flying yielded the feeling of freedom and being above the problems of this life. Perhaps it was another escape from reality. It seemed he would find himself escaping from reality in a lot of ways. I'm not quite sure why, but Dad seemed to love to live on the edge. He loved to take risks. Risks are okay if you know the safety net is out or there is a way to escape from what's about to happen. Risks are okay as long as you remember "Hey I have a family and if I do this it will destroy my family!" His boundaries were nowhere near what they should have been.

This daredevil side was reflective in his military service. When in the Navy, Dad had served as a demolition expert, dismantling ordnance. Somewhere during those days, at the end of World War 2, he got a day of leave, and saw the ammunition dump explode in a fireball just as he was leaving the base. The sailor that had taken his place accidentally detonated a bomb and when Dad saw that explosion, he thought of hell. He said, "God spoke to me and said that's what hell will be like! Preach the gospel and tell men not to go there!" That was his call to preach! So even in the midst of living on the edge he knew the voice of God. Yet had he tuned that voice out?

But now, Dad wasn't preaching, pastoring or praying. Little did I know as he would tell me later, "God never stopped talking to me. He kept giving me messages and kept moving in my heart... but my heart was dark and not responding." Now no longer pastoring, he was trying to make ends meet by crop dusting. Catching a job here and there. He tried to stay busy.

Failure Seems Final

Failure destroys and rips at the fabric of relationships. Husbands and wives stop talking. Children are isolated to their phones and TVs. Food becomes an out. Drugs seem to ease the chaos and allow you to escape the pain. Unfortunately after numerous affairs my Dad had destroyed all the trust between him and Mom.

It's been said sin will take you farther than you want to go and keep you longer than you want to stay and make you pay more than you want to pay. Well Dad did just that. We all did that. We were all paying for his sin. We had gone further than any of us had wanted to go. If only he had stopped.

Perhaps there is still time for you. You can stop before you go on. You can turn around and make a new decision to follow the Lord. It's not too late.

Being the daredevil that he was, I remember Dad crashing his plane on more than one occasion. One plane crash would be enough for most, but I think Dad crashed at least three times and walked away each time. Once while spraying some mesquite he said, "Well, the engine just stopped and I rode it in!" It took the wings off as he crashed through the trees. Another time, he said, "Well, it ran out of gas just short of the runway by a hundred feet." Straight down into the ground it went!

That time he was blinded for two weeks by the poison that had dumped on him but again, he walked away.

He had a great personality, a beautiful smile, and the most handsome set of gray-blue eyes you have ever seen with two deep dimples on each cheek. He was charming, he had a wonderful laugh; I will always miss hearing Dad's laugh. He truly was a great man. Some of his best characteristics contributed to his greatest downfall: his looks, his personality, his abilities to persuade and his sheer love for people.

Before Dad's downfall, back in Olney in the mid-sixties I remember going out many nights with him to see the Army helicopters fly in at low level, practicing for Vietnam. I was just a kid of six or seven but it remains a special memory. They would come in for a landing there at the little runway. We would all ride out and watch as the lights of those choppers came hovering in at low altitude. Cash in our pop bottles at the corner store, at three cents each, buy some cold Cokes and peanut patties and then head out to the landing strip. They would land, talk, and then take off again. It was exciting and something different to do in that little Texas town. With no AC in the house and the cool night breezes it was always fun to go out and watch the helos come in and land. Besides it was just fun being out with Dad.

After Dad got out of the ministry, he was always gone.

Sometimes he was gone for months at a time. I wish I could say Dad left and was out earning money for the family. The truth was Dad didn't help our family very much financially. He was gone! He left. We were on our own. Mom brought in the only real income and she became a single parent from then on. At times Dad would drop in and visit. Sometimes he would even get a short-term job somewhere. But nothing worked, as he was on the run from God!

His failure made our lives so lonely. We lived for his visits. We longed for his visits. We couldn't wait to hear from him, but we became weary of the excuses of why he didn't come home. We began to realize life would never be the same.

Mom

Mom worked as a bookkeeper at an insurance company. She was the rock! She was the constant. She was true north. What would we have done if she had faltered? Thank God she stood strong! It just didn't seem possible that our perfect little life was over and that Dad was gone.

Thank God for that one person who won't quit. Who says, "I don't care what happens, I'm not leaving you!" Where would we have been if Mom had quit? Dad had given up on us but we hadn't given up on him and we hadn't given up on each other. We pressed through, and you have to press through also. Don't let the bad news be <u>the</u> news.

Where's My Dad?

I remember laying in bed many nights crying, "God, why won't my Dad come home? God, make my Dad come home! *I miss my Daddy!* Dad why don't you come home? Where are you? Why don't you love us anymore?" I was so hurt and so alone and I felt so betrayed. I felt like it was my fault.

For long months at a time he would be gone. We struggled to make ends meet. Mom said later that we could have received welfare she just didn't know that we were eligible for it. She said, "I thought it was for poor people!" We were the poor people. We lived on very little and it was okay. We made it. We never missed a meal. Thank God, Mom never quit! She just kept going.

We Had to Keep Going!

That's what you have to do. Keep going. Keep pressing forward. Don't worry about the details. The details will work themselves out. The important thing is keep stepping forward.

Mom was the best cook. She would cook in a Dutch oven and would tell my brother and me every night, "This is it! There's nothing else… eat up… tomorrow is the end of the world." Or so she would make us think. And we did. We "ate that pot empty" every night. Then the next night it was the same speech - and the same results. We cleaned that pot every night.

Even though we had it tough, Mom always made room for others. Several times we took in other family members and some even lived with us. Cousins and aunts at one time or another moved in and Mom helped them all. She was the greatest example of how we live through the stuff. It would have been easy to quit but she didn't.

Those were tough years, '67-'71. Those were the darkest of my childhood years. We didn't attend church much. We would go sometimes, but more than not we would stay home and avoid people. That was Mom's dark time. She was humiliated by Dad's betrayal. I'm sure we were a topic around some tables of gossip, or maybe that's what she feared. We just hid out at the house and lived another life.

At times we did attend. Mom would take us on occasion, but I didn't understand why we didn't go as much as we had before. And the question loomed over my mind all the time. Where was my Dad? Why did he leave us? That question would haunt me for the next nine years.

It wasn't until I was sixteen and attended a revival service back at our old church in Olney that I asked one of those dear old saints, "What happened to my Dad?"

Back to Mayberry

I was so excited to go back to the place where Dad had pastored. This was our Mayberry. It was where life had been perfect. Just 45 minutes from Wichita Falls and yet it was a million miles away. I remember that night, walking in and seeing the pulpit and the red carpet and the smell of the oak woodwork and those large stained glass windows. I didn't expect the answer she gave me. She was one of those sweet old saints. Her words even to this day are like a knife in my heart. Her reaction to my question was one of surprise. She was surprised that I didn't know, and with a thick Texas drawl she replied, "Well Honey, your Father had an affair!"

Everything went dark. It seemed like ringing in my ears. You feel numb from the aftershock. You don't know what to say. The first time you hear the news, you want to run. You can't believe this is real. "No!" your mind screams. Nothing prepared you and yet you suspected the worst was happening but nothing like this. Not for it to be said out loud.

I was shocked! I cried and cried. I walked out of the church...trying not to let anyone know how devastated I was. I was broken, destroyed, wounded, and paralyzed with doubt. How could that be? He was my hero! He was my Dad! Why didn't I see that? How dumb was I that I couldn't see it? But I was a kid. Why didn't someone tell me?

I had said to friends that my Dad was in the ministry and had retired from it. He hadn't retired. He had been thrown out. He had betrayed his calling and I had to see it for what it was. It was shame and we would carry that shame with him.

Dad had backslid and was running from God! I loved him so much and now I could see the missing piece of the puzzle.

When we finally went back to church, the church we chose was not the main-street church. It was a new church out near the air base. It was out in the country and a new pastor came to the tiny church just after we started attending. Dan Heil was his name. He came with his lovely wife Jerri and three daughters: Pam, Janet and Danielle. He was young and energetic. He was an amazing pastor. His love was so great for everyone he met. He had a passion for prayer and the church started growing. I was just 11 years old.

A New Beginning

Thank God for new beginnings. In the midst of your bad news, thank God for new friends and new places and the new God places in your life. The new place where God will make himself real to you. We needed a new beginning. We needed a new start.

This new pastor was amazing. A few weeks after he started pastoring there, he had a young Vietnam War-veteran come and preach. His face was severely scarred, but he had a powerful way of preaching the gospel. His name was Dave Roever. Dave had been seriously injured in Vietnam a few years earlier, as a result of an exploding hand grenade. I loved hearing Dave preach. I could listen to him all day. His stories came alive to me. I laughed and cried all the way through his testimony. It was powerful. He spoke of his scars and how Christ was helping him. I hurt so much for him and thought how Christ had been scarred for me. I accepted Jesus as my personal Savior in that revival. A few years later I was baptized and soon after that filled with the powerful Holy Spirit.

Dan Heil was an amazing pastor. He loved me and became like a dad to me. He knew the story of my dad and reached out to me. Little did I know then that he would later become my father-in-law. His youngest daughter Danielle became my life partner. I love her so much and she will always be my best friend!

With all the amazing love and enthusiasm he carried, he never felt adequate as a preacher, but no one could hold a candle to his loving way of pastoring people. I still maintain he has the best hugs in the world. That's how he built such a dynamic church. He put his arms around people and brought them close and loved them into the Kingdom. We had such great services in that little church on a hill.

I wish I could say at salvation that all of my problems left, but they didn't. I still missed the love of my Dad. I still longed for a relationship with him and hoped some day we could be together again. I remembered many days of the simpler times chasing Dad. I remember him letting me catch him; I loved him so much! Oh how I wish he was there to let me chase him again. I would catch him and hug him with all my strength. I would never let him go!

In those days, it was common for me to walk to church. It wasn't close, but many times, after lunch on Sundays, I would tell my momma, "Mom, I want to go back to church!" She would say, "Well son, there's not much gas in the car and I'll be going back up there in a bit for the night service. Why don't you wait?" Now mind you, gas was 35 cents a gallon… I would tell her, "That's okay, I'll just walk!" She would ask, "How are you going to get in?" I would tell her, "No big deal Mom, I'll pick the pastor's outside door!" I could do it with a comb or knife. In those days, the pastor would show up for evening church, and many times, I would be sitting at his desk or praying at the altars in the church.

God will always hear the heart of a hungry person. He will always feed that person with his fresh love. I felt so unloved and He filled that void in my life.

Called to Preach!

It was January 1, 1973, when it happened. It was an evening watch night service, at the old Evangel Temple in Wichita Falls. I was called to preach. Mike Evans was the evangelist. He was a tall man, a Messianic Jew with a powerful, prophetic voice. That night, during the altar time, I was "slain under the power," as we called it. I laid there under the cloud of glory for what seemed like forever. We sang into the night and celebrated the new year. For me it was a new life of even greater hopes and dreams. I remember getting home early in the morning and telling Mom about what had happened. I told her something was telling me to read about David's life, in the Bible. She said, "Well, start reading in First Samuel."

That night, I went to my room and began to read in First Samuel. Mom knew what she was doing. She knew the hunger I had for the Lord! She could see the passion for

His house and His altars! I remember reading one chapter thinking I had blazed a new trail, and how awesome it was I had read one chapter... how funny. Then the Holy Spirit spoke to my heart and said, "Read on!" so I did! Then it happened. In verse 35 of Chapter 2, He spoke to me...

"Then I will raise up for Myself a faithful priest who shall do according to what is in My heart and in My mind. I will build him a sure house, and he shall walk before My anointed forever."
(1 Samuel 2:35 NKJV)

Faithfulness, His heart, His mind and a sure house! Those were the things that jumped out at me; I was desirous of walking before Him as His anointed forever! It wasn't David... it wasn't Samuel... It wasn't David or Samuel... It was me! It was the boy given to the Lord as a child. The barren mother praying for a child. A boy dedicated to God! Given because he was given to hopeful parents! That was me!

"Mom, Mom, wake up! The Lord just spoke to me about a call on my life!" I ran in and told my mom! She sat there and listened to me. I wonder what she thought? Have you ever hoped you could go back and see a scene again in your life because it was so amazing and wonderful? Oh how I wish I could see her face again as I rattled on about the night and the powerful service and what had just happened, as I had read the Bible. I had so many wonderful nights talking to my mom. We often sat on her bed and relived a wonderful church service or discussed a scripture the Lord had shown me.

The boy Samuel had heard the Lord speak to him and he ran to the prophet! I ran to my Mom, my mentor, my precious *Momma* to tell her the great news! The woman who prayed and asked the Lord for a child.

"Now the Lord came and stood and called as at other times, "Samuel! Samuel!" And Samuel answered, "Speak, for Your servant hears."
(I Samuel 3:10 NKJV)

Mom always encouraged me in the call. She would remind me as I grew up. "Michael, remember you are called to preach!" It was that gentle reminder from a loving Mom. What a great example! What a loving lady God gave me to mentor me and lead me to the ministry.

But I Missed My Dad

I wanted him to be proud of me! I wanted him in my life! I needed him! I hoped he would come home. I longed for a phone call! In those days, we didn't have cell phones and social media. A person could get lost if they wanted and a kid had no way of contacting a parent if they chose to disappear. And he did. For months we would hear nothing. No phone calls, no mail, no messages. He could have died and we wouldn't have known where he was. I think back now and think how selfish that was. We needed his love more than life. But Dad had checked out. He was gone. He was living on an island of "leave me alone." He was hurting and had lost his love for the ministry. It seemed he had lost his love for us as well.

One night I ran away from home. It was after a pretty big fight between my brother and me. I went to the only safe place on earth. I went to the church. It was safe. It was where I felt love and I knew the Lord was there. So many times before I had gone there and never needed a key. I could use a comb or pocketknife and break into the pastor's office. But on this particular night, I couldn't break in. I was locked out. Many times I had broken in and called my pastor from his desk phone. "Pastor Heil, I need you! Yes sir – no, I'm not home. I'm at the church! I'm in your office! Yes sir, I'll wait right here!" He would come up there and be a Dad He would put his big arms around me and hug me and tell me he was there and that God loved me and was going to take care of me. But not tonight. Tonight, I sat there alone. I walked around the parking lot crying. I cried and cried! I was filled with despair and hurt. If my Dad was here he would defend me and make Jim behave. He would take care of me and help me.

Not being able to get in the church and having no way to call anyone I retreated to the only place that I could get into, a church bus. So I opened the door and climbed in and sat down on the front seat behind the driver's seat and kept crying. I asked the Lord, "Where's my Dad? Why doesn't he come home? Why doesn't he love me? Why doesn't he want to be with us?" I was 14; I needed my Dad. It hurt so bad. And at that very moment... a miracle happened! All these years I had been chasing my. I had cried myself to sleep night after night. I had prayed and asked the Lord why won't my Dad come home? And then it happened... my Dad walked in...

Sitting there all alone in that old church bus... it was as if the bus door swung open and standing there in all of His glory was my Abba "Daddy" God! At that moment He walked in! Not physically... no, I didn't see Him... but He was there. It was as if His sweet presence came into that old church bus. The aroma of that bus changed from the smell of old dusty vintage seats to the living presence of God the Father. He came in and sat down beside me on that bus seat. Just as He had appeared to Abraham on a mountainside and Moses at a bush and David at a stream... He was there with me... He put his arms around me and said, "I'm here! I'll be your Father! I'll be your Dad! I'll be there for you! I'll be there at your ball game and your drama production. I'll be there when you're down and when you succeed. I'll be there for the rest of your life. I'll be proud of you and I'll stand there on the sidelines when you are looking for your Dad. I'll be there! And I'll be proud of you! You're my boy!" That night, God the Father became my Dad. He was there! He became my Dad! My Abba Father! I had searched and searched for my Dad, and that night, HE caught me. He lovingly walked into my world and became so real. It wasn't a vision. It was an inward awakening of His holy presence in my heart. He loved me and would never leave me. It was His arms that reached around me and held me that night. It was an amazing evening of crying and pouring out my heart. It was an evening that I will never forget.

"For you did not receive the spirit of bondage again to fear, but you received the Spirit of adoption by whom we cry out, "Abba, Father." (Romans 8:15 NKJV)

"And because you are sons, God has sent forth the Spirit of His Son into your hearts, crying out, "Abba, Father!" (Galatians 4:6 NKJV)

"A father of the fatherless, a defender of widows, is God in His holy habitation." (Psalm 68:5 NKJV)

It was an evening of transformation for me. The truth of His love and His fatherhood to me was now a new revelation. If my earthly father had forsaken me, then now my Heavenly Father would defend me and be there for me. He would take care of me and He would help me.

Many times in my life, I've gone back to that night. I've remembered that evening in the old church bus. It struck a chord in my heart that nothing can change. He saw me and heard my cry and came and helped me. He became my Abba! I love Him! With all my hurt and pain He was there. When no one else could reach me He did. When it felt as though the world was crashing in, my Heavenly Father loved me. He loves you! He knows where you are. He knows your hurt and your pain!

"Victor Numquam Usque"

Don't quit! Don't give up! Don't let whatever it is destroy you! Whether it's a parent who's forsaken you, or an illness, or a spouse who's left you... or your own personal failure... your Father is here right now. He loves you! You are worth salvaging. You are worth saving. Get up and get going! He loves you! Feel His arms going around you holding you up. His loving arms are everlasting and will help you make it.

There have been many times in my life when I've wanted to quit, when I've wanted to run. But I've remembered He was watching me and reminding me He loved me and was proud of me and was saying, "Never quit! Never give up! Never run away! I'm with you and I will never forsake you!"

Many times before speaking in a church service I've

declared to the Lord, "I want you to be proud of me tonight! I don't want to disappoint you today! Let me do well!" What a joy it has been to know HE was watching on the sidelines and HE was proud of the steps of faith I would take.

Many years later I spoke with Dad and he told me that during that season in his life, when he was running from God, God never left him. He continued to get sermons. He knew the Lord was reaching out to him and loving him. Even though he had nowhere to preach those sermons, God never stopped speaking to him.

My Dad and I never had the relationship I had longed for. He died in July of 2010. It was as we were struggling to complete the building; I found myself rushing back and forth to his bedside, six hours away, trying to be a good son, and a faithful Pastor. Neither he nor Mom ever saw the completed project. But I believe my Heavenly Father celebrated with me and rejoiced with us as we eventually completed the impossible.

A Good Good Father!

Not only does God love us but as we are chasing our Daddy, our Abba Daddy, Father God is chasing us. For my Dad, his Abba Father was chasing Him! Just as your Abba is chasing you! HE loves you enough to give His only Son! So…

Don't quit! Never give up! Hang in there! Ask the Lord to help you today! Let Him step into your problem. Whether it's a problem you've created or a problem that you've been thrust into... this is your day for Him to deliver you and for Him to show Himself strong!

Ask Him Today to Help You.

This book is about my journey. I wanted to quit! I wanted to give up! I wanted to turn and run but He would not let me! I'm praying the remaining pages will reach you and help you realize that as He helped me He will help you and reach you wherever you are.

One of the great things I've learned about the Lord is He never gives up! I give up. I quit. He never quits. He always loves. He always pursues with forgiveness and restoration. I have to be willing to receive what He has. I have to be willing to see when He walks in, and I must accept His loving care and His righteous rebukes. Sometimes we need to repent before we can receive what He wants to give us and sometimes we have to open up to receive His healing. I'm so thankful He never gives up.

There's a Latin term I've adopted as a creed: **"Victor Numquam Usque!"** Translated, it means "A winner never gives up!" It's written from the future imperative tense. In other words, it is the declaration that it may not appear as yet to be seen in the natural but it is a fact that you will win! You have already won! Christ defeated the powers of darkness on the cross and celebrated it at the resurrection! So rejoice in the Lord and in His power. And remember…

A Winner
Never Gives Up!

Victor Numquam Usque!

Chapter 1
He Never Gives Up!

Just like a loving father - He never gives up on us!

"For you did not receive the spirit of bondage again to fear, but you received the Spirit of adoption by whom we cry out, "Abba, Father." (Romans 8:15 NKJV)

"And because you are sons, God has sent forth the Spirit of His Son into your hearts, crying out, "Abba, Father!" (Galatians 4:6 NKJV)

"A father of the fatherless, a defender of widows, is God in His holy habitation." (Psalm 68:5 NKJV)

Discussion Questions

Have you ever wanted to quit?
What discourages you most: people, events or yourself?
God wants relationship with us as a Father.
What would every father want for their child?

What's your greatest dream?

_____

_____

_____

_____

What are the things you will never give up?

Family, Marriage, Walk with the Lord, Healing... etc.

1. _____
2. _____
3. _____
4. _____
5. _____
6. _____
7. _____
8. _____
9. _____
10. _____

"Victor Numquam Usque!"

Never Give Up!

Chapter 2
His Plan is Always Better

We've all made plans that didn't turn out the way we had hoped they would. Too often I've found my plans somehow don't work out no matter how hard I tried to keep that from happening. Whether it was a new ministry idea, or a stock tip, or a new business someone was so eager for me to try. Usually my best-laid plans never quite work out the way His Plans work out.

It was a few years after we completed Crossroads Fellowship's first phase. We had somehow "made it" and I was feeling good about life. I was on my way home from a wonderful day of victory. The rain was washing over my windshield and all I could think of was how great God had been to us. It was our annual missions convention weekend and we had had a miraculous day. The goals were up and it seemed we had turned the corner in our darkest night.

As the windshield wipers thumped back and forth, I heard that all-too-familiar sound, a text coming through on my cell phone. It was one of our Master's Commission students. "Pray for my Dad!" it read.

His Dad was a pastor. The rest of the text read: "If you could call him and encourage him?" What wasn't written was the hurt this student felt for his Dad. The young man was an armor bearer for me. Dozens of times, every week, he would ask me, "Is there anything I can do for you, Pastor?"

It was my turn to give someone encouragement. I had wanted to quit. I had almost quit.

I could tell he was hurting for his dad. He had told me a few weeks before that his dad was discouraged. He had been in the ministry over 30 years; he had given the best years of his life to his church, and instead of growing, his church was full of grumbling, back-biting saints. He had never had a pay increase during his entire 14 years of pastoring that church. A year before, this same pastor had been to see me during my dark days while building Crossroads.

Thank God for the family members who won't quit on you. Thank God for the loving family that pulls you through the hell you're crawling through.

My Plan

The story seems surreal. What was supposed to have been an easy build for Crossroads ended up being the most stressful time of my life. In 2004, we had purchased 28 gorgeous acres on a future beltway around the city of Houston. In 2007, we had sold the old church property, for $3 million and paid for the new property. We had received $3.5 million in funding from our local bank to construct this wonderful new facility. Construction began in early 2008. With approval from the church, we moved forward with the project. However, the amount of money to complete what we wanted to build would cost us millions of dollars more. At one of our minister functions, we came across another lending institution that assured us they would help us complete the project. They had the money and they would be there when we needed them.

We went through their vigorous reviews, secured a letter of approval, and received a promise that they would step in and complete this project. Unfortunately, after we received a letter of commitment and went through a financial campaign, this institution pulled away from us during the financial meltdown of 2008-09. We were already deep into the project before we knew this. In fact we had spent all of the $6.5 million on the new project before we found out this new group was not going to perform. We were told to go ahead and when it came time for their money they would be ready and for us not to worry.

Before getting into this project a wise old preacher prophetically told me, "You'll be all right, as long as the economy holds up." It didn't. The worst economic recession since the Great Depression of the 1930s hit

America. The financial group dropped us and left us "holding the bag."

Disaster!

I remember screaming on the phone at one of the representatives of this organization, "What? You're not going to hold up your end of the bargain? You said you were going to do this... what am I going to do?" There were a lot of those conversations. A lot of anger! A lot of sleepless nights! A lot of questions why!

We were $6.5 million into a building project and we needed another $1.7 million just to get into the building. We were making payments on $3.5 million and I was sick. I wanted to die. My builder had done his part. The church had done their part. My bank had loaned us the money but I was in this chasm of despair. This new group had left us and there was nothing I could do. It was as though we were swimming midstream and had no way to go back and no way to move forward. I was drowning in despair.

Unable to move forward, we were at a standstill. Owing millions, and with no way to get the project finished, weeds began to grow around God's vision.

Chaos and Confusion

Our future church sat empty and vacant, and nothing was moving forward. With this huge embarrassment growing every day, I began to retreat. I tried to believe but to no avail. It had gotten so bad... I didn't want to see anyone. I didn't want to attend anything. If I heard "When are you getting into your new building?" one more time, I believe I would have hurt someone. I was one huge ball of festering hurt inside. We were at a standstill... Our building was covered in weeds and nothing was happening. We owed millions and we were meeting in a school with no way of completing construction. Our monthly mortgage payment was $30,000. Plus we were paying the school around $3,000 in monthly rent and several thousand more for storages. We sold our old property, having left that great security, and invested all in the new project, but it would not be finished. I kept asking myself all these questions: "Why did you sell?" "Why did you move?" "Did you really hear from God?" But in deep agony I couldn't tell anyone how alone I felt. Only a few very close friends knew the depths of my dilemma. I gained more and more weight. I was in a pit of depression, and I couldn't climb out.

The pain of what I was experiencing was so difficult. I had given my all. I had believed and yet where was God? I had never felt so alone. Although people tried to console me, nothing helped. I pulled the mask over my face to go to church and preach. I learned how to smile and not show that inside I was dying.

In The Fire!

My faith was in the fire. It was being purged of any pride that could be left. Where do you practice this kind of faith? Pride has to leave. It can't stay. I did not want this cup. I just wanted to finish this building and move on with my life. Every scripture about believing God was my constant prayer, and my course was set: Mike Allard must die. It was then I remembered what James said,

"God opposes the proud but shows favor to the humble." 7 Submit yourselves, then, to God. Resist the devil, and he will flee from you. 8 Come near to God and He will come near to you. Wash your hands, you sinners, and purify your hearts, you double-minded. 9 Grieve, mourn and wail. Change your laughter to mourning and your joy to gloom. 10 Humble yourselves before the Lord, and He will lift you up."
(James 4: 6b-10 NIV)

I didn't feel like I had done anything wrong... except believe. You may be in the same place. You've stretched your faith. You've trusted God. I felt let down. Sometimes you can feel that you've literally done all you can... but have you?

I had exercised faith and I had trusted this organization to step in as it had claimed. There was nothing I could do now. It was a humbling time. It was a storm to say the least. Too bad Job didn't have a friend like James to turn to. I don't know though - perhaps if James had walked up and said those lines about humbling myself I might have punched him. My laughter was gone. Every day was a terrible, dreaded experience. The mere sliver of sleep I managed to get each day was the best time of the day.

Go Deeper

It was during those days however, that I found out what kind of a man I was. My faith was in the fire and I wondered if I would survive. I asked God, "Why? Why hadn't you shown me? Where are you now God? Didn't you see this? Were you talking to me and I just didn't listen?"

I wondered if I had truly heard from God. I questioned myself about everything. There was no pride, no self-esteem; I was only a wounded soul living in a body.

During that time I found that faith really isn't about feelings. It had to get to where I no longer questioned, I just stood in my faith. At the same time I found myself standing in that building - a deserted vision with weeds and debris; scattered pieces of construction material strewn around those unfinished dreams and darkness. Everything was just dark; nothing seemed real. I couldn't believe I was at this place in my life.

You feel like that when you want to quit. You are overwhelmed by the chaos of it all. It seems as though it can't get worse and then something else happens. Death happens. Darkness happens. There is no joy. No singing. It's just all gone.

A few very close friends reached out to me and tried to help me. This student's Dad was one who asked me in those dark days, "Are you okay?" I remember him dropping by on occasion to check on his son and he would poke his head in my office and ask, "How's it going?" In retrospect, I'm not sure if he was really interested, or if he was just a curiosity seeker. Sometimes people want to slow down and see how bad is this accident.

I'm reminded of a bad Charles Barkley impersonation: "turrable." It was just terrible. (But I didn't say that.) I lied. I told him great... or it could be better... Or I would tell him of the latest hope in a new idea to get the project moving again. But all the while my heart screamed, "What if that doesn't work either?"

Now it was my turn, to return to him those precious words he had given to me. I called him and said words that every pastor knows so well, "I know what you're going through," and "I'm sorry." Those words resonated through my soul. I didn't want to sound hollow or uncaring. I truly was concerned and I had appreciated the couple of times he had checked on me. Now it was my turn.

"You're going to make it! Your success is not determined on whether they receive your message. It's up to you to follow the will of God; they may play a part in that, but God directs." I told him, "If that election doesn't go your way, they may be doing you a big favor." I was mad for him. I thanked him for being there for me and I could tell that he was in a dark place… there was this pause of silence. He was wounded and hurting.

Too many around us are wounded and hurting. The enemy's job is to steal, kill and destroy. The devil is good at his job. He's been stealing again, he's been killing again and he's destroying everything he can.

God's Plan

Let me remind you that God's plan is better. During tumultuous times, it seemed Israel's future was all but over. But during this time, God gave the prophet Jeremiah a great promise for His people. If this promise was good enough for those rebellious Israelites then it's good enough for God's children today. Get ahold of this enduring word, and let it be your promise today!

"For I know the thoughts that I think toward you, says the Lord, thoughts of peace and not of evil, to give you a future and a hope. 12 Then you will call upon Me and go and pray to Me, and I will listen to you. 13 And you will seek Me and find Me, when you search for Me with all your heart. 14 I will be found by you…"
(Jeremiah 29:11-14a ESV)

A Winner
Never Gives Up!

Chapter 2
His Plan is Always Better

My plans rarely turn out the way I hope.

"For I know the thoughts that I think toward you, says the Lord, thoughts of peace and not of evil, to give you a future and a hope. 12 Then you will call upon Me and go and pray to Me, and I will listen to you. 13 And you will seek Me and find Me, when you search for Me with all your heart. 14 I will be found by you…" (Jeremiah 29:11-14a ESV)

Discussion Questions

Have you ever planned something and it failed?
Has your life had some turns you didn't expect?

What are things God uses to guide us?

_____
_____
_____
_____
_____
_____
_____
_____

What positive things have happened since you accepted Christ?

No More Sin, New Friends, Finding Life… etc.

1. _____
2. _____
3. _____
4. _____
5. _____
6. _____
7. _____
8. _____
9. _____
10. _____

"Wait on Him!"

Never Give Up!

Chapter 3
He Speaks Through Storms

I wanted to die. At least then, it would be over. I wanted it to all go away. Is there a point where you hate the vision? Is there a point where you hope that it will die and leave you alone? How did I get here?

The Ministry

It all began on May 27, 2001, when I was elected as the Lead Pastor of Crossroads Fellowship, formerly known as Greens Bayou Assembly of God. I had previously served as the Youth/Children's Pastor from 1982-1990.

During those days, Reverend J.P. Granberry had served as pastor. We had a great ministry at the church. God's favor upon the ministry had been abundant; we had experienced affirmation and growth, and Danielle and I were invited back to pastor the congregation in 2001. Brother Granberry was one of my spiritual fathers. He was a wonderful, happy pastor; a loving friend and mentor; and a man who truly taught me the value of prayer. For the spiritual and life lessons Rev. Granberry taught me, I will forever be indebted. I will always remember those days as some of my very best days. It felt so good to go back home. It had become that – home. We longed to return to the fellowship we had known and to the many loving friends.

I had grown so close to this congregation and they had given so much to Danielle and me. In 1982, when we first came to the church, we lived in a little trailer donated by a church member. It was a great time in our lives. We had only one child then, Joshua. He was one. Later Michael David would arrive and then Lacey. Financially, it was probably our most trying time but we made it through. It was just what you did. We were in the ministry, and we were in the will of God. We loved every minute of it. We were earning our stripes. It didn't seem unfair or unreasonable. It wasn't easy, but we didn't expect it to be easy. I worked "side jobs" and Danielle babysat for people in the church, just to make ends meet. On occasion, we did janitorial work for the church. Eventually, with the church growth we experienced, our salary increased, thanks to the generosity of Crossroads. Those were some of the greatest days of our ministry, and some of the most trying as well. Don't get me wrong - we went through some excruciating trials during those early years. But isn't that the ministry, a mixture of trials and blessings by having your faith tried and your faith approved? James said, "Blessed is the one who perseveres under trial because, having stood the test, that person will receive the crown of life that the Lord has promised to those who love him."
(James 1:12 NIV)

What a Mess

How could I have gotten this great church into such a mess? If people only knew how alone I felt, surely they would gather around me and help me... but nothing seemed to help. I felt like it would destroy the church if people knew the mess we were in. I felt like such a failure. During that time we even fell behind in support for our missionaries. Our priorities were out of order. We did everything we could to stay afloat and said very little to the congregation about how bad it really was. Ultimately that was my decision. I wondered if I shared the depth of the situation whether people would feel such despair that they would choose to leave. Not feeling as though I could confide in those who loved me so much, I retreated further into myself.

I felt lost in a vicious storm. Somewhere along the way, instead of getting out, I had made the decision to stay and ride out the torrent. Instead of choosing a safer path I had somehow led my flock into one of the biggest disasters a pastor could face. How could I have been so stupid? Why did I step out in such a reckless manner? I wanted to quit but I couldn't!

There are so many great moments that make up a life: birthdays, family gatherings, weddings, vacations, holidays, remembrances, and so many other special days. I have always enjoyed life. There are so many special moments and occasions: date night with Danielle, a great service at church, hunting excursions with my boys, working on an old car, or simply being out with friends. However, now I felt like Job. "I loathed my life..." (Job 10:1a)

How would we make it through this? How would we get to the other side of this pit? As I reflect back upon the valleys and the mountains, perhaps it can now help you to survive your storm! Maybe my experience will encourage you to not give up and run and hide.

I'm sure Job wanted to quit. Everything was gone. He had lost it all. I'm sure more than once he told himself, "I quit!" Maybe you've said those words, "I quit." It's okay to quit... at least that's what Pastor Tommy Barnett always says, "You can quit, just don't." I love that! I remember hearing that on this journey. It wasn't a personal call from a spiritual giant. It was simply one of those times. I sat in a conference and I needed to hear one thing. Tommy said it, and I'll never forget it. "You can quit, just don't."

There's usually never just one thing that will cause you to quit. It's usually several things or a growing mountain of things. Things you wished would just stop... and then it's the straw that breaks the camel's back. Maybe it's a person's words; a phone call; a look; a bit of news; or the timing of an event. Whatever it is, you just can't imagine going forward. It's okay to say to yourself, "I quit..." Tell it to your dog. Tell it to a close friend. Tell it and then just don't do it. Refuse to quit! Look the devil in the eye and say, I'm moving forward! I'm pressing ahead! I will never give up! "Numquam Usque!" NEVER GIVE UP!

I had never really enjoyed reading the Book of Job. In my reading list, it was somewhere after the obituaries. It seemed like a waste of paper in the Bible. Who wants to hear a guy whine? He questions God? I mean - really - who gets away with that? It seems as though it served Job right to get everything zapped if he was going to have that kind of attitude.

Well, every day I felt more and more like Job. I was becoming his modern-day twin.

When Job said he loathed his life, it now made sense to me. *I understand you Brother Job. Amen! Preach it!* All of his children were gone; everything he owned was stolen or destroyed; and on top of that, his friends told him... "You must have sinned because God has forsaken you." And his wife said, "Why don't you go ahead and curse God and die?"

Message in the Storm

I can't think or imagine how dark life could have been for Brother Job. How do you lose a child and survive? Or how do you recover when everything is stolen and then the one person you hope will encourage you tells you to curse God. Job was robbed. Job got a bad deal. No, he got the worse deal. It was the storm of a lifetime. It was the storm of 10 lifetimes. Yet through it all Job blessed the Lord.

At the conclusion of Job's trials came a message: "Then the LORD spoke to Job out of the storm..." (Job 38:1a)

The Holy Spirit has used a lot of things to draw my attention in order to build a sermon: a certain Scripture; a song; a picture; a poem; a story; a moment with my children – always the Holy Spirit's whisper. But in this case, God used a storm to speak to me!

God spoke to me from the storm I was facing. I didn't know it at the time. I couldn't hear it because my own screaming drowned out the voices. I had to get quiet, and I had to stop and listen. That's the hard part. When the eye of the storm was directly over me and it got quiet – that's when I just went outside to see how still it really was.

He is trying to speak to you today. He loves you so much! He cares for you! He hasn't forgotten you! He has been there every step of the way... It's that still small voice in your heart that's telling you right now, "I LOVE YOU!" You're His child. Just feel His arms wrap around you today.

Danielle says that I have selective hearing. She can be telling me one thing and the next minute it's as if I never heard what she said. It's reminiscent of Charlie Brown's teacher; all I can hear is, "wah wah wah wah wah…" Maybe I didn't hear it… or perhaps I tuned her out. I hate it when that happens because inevitably I have to go back and say, "Hey, what did you say?" The truth is, I heard it but I just chose not to listen. There is something about listening and hearing. We hear a lot of things - but we don't listen.

Are You Listening?

Job, are you listening? Mike, are you listening? Are you? Is He using something to get your attention? Even though the world is falling apart around you? He is speaking. "I'm with you. I will never leave you! Don't quit! Don't give up!"

The Prophet Elijah found himself in a cave alone, afraid, and questioning his worth. Have you ever questioned yourself? Have you sat in a cave of hurt and despair and wondered, "Where do I go from here," and then God whispered to you? For Elijah, it wasn't in the earthquake and it wasn't in the fire but it was in that still small voice… "Are you listening?"

Perhaps Elijah heard, "What are you running from? If the Lord is for you, who can be against you?" That's just my guess. The message God had for Elijah has been left out. The tone has been left in. God's tone is soft in the storm. He is not trying to get your attention over the fire and the earthquake. His tone is not blaring and violent. It's soft and gentle. It's meek and lowly. He understands how worn out you are and how you simply need to rest.

The words God spoke to Elijah were not recorded and written in the Bible for us to read, but we know that he recognized that the still small voice was from the Lord. And that God does speak to us. His tone and His love are unending and never-changing.

I believe God was there all the time and desired to speak to Job. Day after day, his tender voice was speaking… Job wasn't listening. God had been trying to get Job's attention, just as God was trying to get my attention during my storm.

How many times have we ventured off in our own direction? God was leading us in another direction yet we chose not to listen. Or maybe we're like the disciples. We are exactly where Christ wants us… out in the middle of a storm-tossed sea… just so He can show you once more how great His power really is.

Was it the lightning? Was it the wind? Can you picture

Job, sitting out hearing the thunder crash? The Bible says, "God spoke to Job out of the storm..." (Job 38:1) The first time I pictured this I saw this great old painting in my mind of this aged old man peering through the clouds. Perhaps the picture should be a loving picture of Christ sitting there with you. He is holding you, with His arms around your shoulders, telling you, "I'm here." It'll be okay.

God Speaks Through Storms

God spoke to Job out of the storm. Was it that he was His child and He would never forsake him? Perhaps it was that no weapon formed against him would prosper? Maybe it was one of those crashing thunderbolt sounds that echoed through Job's heart that said, "Are you kidding me Job? You actually think that I would leave you? You are my son, my child, my love... I would even send my Son to save you... Job, I love you." Isn't that what every father tells his son in the middle of life's worst moments? When you just don't know how to move forward... and there's that hand on your shoulder... you look around and those tender eyes look at you and He says, "I'm here. You're going to make it. I love you son, more than you know."

The Psalmist said it perfectly, "I am overwhelmed with troubles..." (Psalm 88:3 NIV)

When I look back I can't help but think of things I could have done differently. We could have raised more money before we built; we could have paid off more debt, having been more aware of the economy; we could have listened to others; we could have taken more time to think some decisions through; and we could have chosen another financial group. I wish I had a "do-over" for some of those days. My reactions to bad news still haunt me. I feel as though I failed on many of those days. Night after night, I went home defeated and nothing good was accomplished in my reactions.

I longed for just days of nothing. I wanted so badly to experience a day of no bad news. A day of a little good news would've allowed me not to feel so overwhelmed.

I wonder if Job also had similar thoughts in his place of sickness, scraping his boils... remembering earlier days, holding his children, laughing? I can just imagine how he felt: alone, confused, depressed, angry and perhaps just plain ol' mad! I remember being so overwhelmed with shame. I thought it was unbearable. The delay in building was killing me a little more every day. My self-confidence was at an all-time low. I loathed my life. It was all I could do to minister.

Giving Birth to Something New!

From the time I knew we were in trouble to the time I

really fell on my knees and began the greatest journey of my life was around nine months. That sounds horrible. Yes I prayed during those nine months but I didn't determine to climb out... and that I would not give up until I had made it through. During that season, God birthed something new inside of me. I remember laying on the cold parking lot of the church crying the prayer Jesus cried on the cross, "My God, My God, why have you forsaken me?" At the time, I really felt abandoned.

At the time, I couldn't confide in my church's Board of Advisors. I couldn't confide in my staff. No friend knew; no one except my wife knew the depth of hurt I was experiencing. I was so embarrassed. My pride was shredded. Danielle saw my depression. I gained 80 pounds. My stress level was over the top! I retreated more and more into a black hole of hurt. She did as much as she could, but I was in a deep, dark place. I hated ministers' meetings. I couldn't stand hearing those words, "When's the church going to be through?" I remember telling them "Soon," and I didn't have a clue. Through all of that, God did guard my life. When I knew the financing was gone and that we would not have the money to finish the main complex, we began to look at every plan possible. Every day seemed like another day of trying to see how we could make this work or how could we make that work? Every day I felt like a hunter checking his traps to see if anything was working. Whatever might work, I would gladly go in that direction.

God was birthing a new church in me. I had sought to enact my vision and my plan. It was what I thought it was going to be and yet He had a greater plan. Your dark days could be God birthing a new you. When a child is brought into this world, there's a powerful process that takes place. The conception, growing, development and maturing of a new baby inside to labor and delivery. God's got to get what He wants first *inside* of you. Then He has to get that *outside* of you. But first, His powerful presence has to begin to grow every day in you!

I felt alone! I felt He had left but He was right there with me! He hadn't abandoned me! He had promised He wouldn't leave me. He was watching me grow in faith. He was watching me slowly become the man of God that He wanted me to be!

In the midst of that storm He did speak to me. He spoke, "Peace be still!" He spoke, "I will never leave you nor forsake you!" He spoke, "You are my child!" He spoke, "No weapon formed against you will prosper!" He spoke and revealed His mighty arm to me again and again.

If you're in the midst of the greatest storm of your life, listen! There is a voice speaking to you. It may not be very loud right now, but it's His voice. It's His message for you. He loves you and He believes in you. He hasn't forgotten you! Hang in there! Don't give up! Don't quit! It'll be worth it! Hang around, just to see how it all works out, because it will!

Let His Holy Presence Birth Something "NEW" Through The Storm.

Victor Numquam Usque!

Chapter 3
He Speaks Through Storms

God has used difficulties to get my attention.

The Psalmist said it perfectly, "I am overwhelmed with troubles..." (Psalm 88:3 NIV)

"Blessed is the one who perseveres under trial because, having stood the test, that person will receive the crown of life that the Lord has promised to those who love him." (James 1:12 NIV)

"Then the LORD spoke to Job out of the storm..." (Job 38:1a)

Discussion Questions

Have you been overwhelmed by something?
What's your first reaction to troublesome storms?
Do you get upset, do you get mad or do you pray?

What difficulties has God used to speak to you?

Sickness, job loss, death, divorce... etc.

_____
_____
_____

_____

_____

_____

What positive things have happened since the storm came?

New Friends, Divine Provision, People I've Helped... etc.

1. _____
2. _____
3. _____
4. _____
5. _____
6. _____
7. _____
8. _____
9. _____
10. _____

"Don't Quit!

Never Give Up!

Chapter 4
He Carries Me Through...

"Surely He has borne our griefs and carried our sorrows..." (Isaiah 53:4 NKJV)

So a good friend asked me, "How did you heal? What was the process that God took you through to get you to the other side?" That's not a light question. It probably has many levels to understand for any minister who has gone through a cataclysmic disruption in his or her life. In the process of looking back, I've found a lot of things I didn't notice along the way. These are stones and markers that have built my faith. Now I'm walking down the path just remembering. Perhaps a few of my discoveries can help you.

I Wanted to End It All!

One of the most difficult times in the journey was the time I wanted to end it all. I had literally driven six hours to my Mom's home... went to her guest room... closed the door... got in bed... pulled the covers over my head and wanted to die. I had had it. Done! Finished! Stop the world - I'm getting off!

It seemed greater than grief. It seemed like grief and sorrow mixed with anger! Anger at myself! Anger at God!

Anger at everything! It wasn't fair! It was the loneliest time of my life!

Who can reach you? Who would help you? David said, "My friends and companions avoid me because of my wounds..." (Psalm 38:11a NIV)

Who wants to be with a guy who no one knows how to comfort... or what to say? I didn't even want to be with me.

Perhaps you've had a moral failure. Perhaps you've had a life-changing sickness. Perhaps you've been thrown into a situation for which you had no way of escaping its grasp, and you did nothing wrong. Maybe you made some bad business decisions or a relationship went south. Now you're crushed and full of grief. Sorrow fills your every thought. You're angry at everything.

It reminds me of the locust shells I used to see as a kid. You remember, the hull of the insect, after he climbs out and there is only discarded skin. Sometimes you feel like, "Oh God, breathe life back into me! Revive this shell of the man I once was."

Hear me! Don't give up on yourself and don't give up on God! If you're the friend or relative... don't give up on them. Don't let their obvious attempts of pushing you away convince you that they don't need help. They're screaming inside for someone to reach into their pit and pull them out. Don't let them hurt alone. Stay there with them. They need you!

Failure

It was October 7, 2009, and two nice-looking 30-something year-old men had requested a visit at my temporary office. Their straightforward comments stung me hard. They said, "We are embarrassed of the church." They used our children's ministry as an excuse to leave. They left me with the thought that I had mismanaged the money on the building and they were ashamed to drive by and see all the weeds growing in front of the church. They couldn't understand how I had gotten the church in such bad shape. These were the very people I was trying to reach. They were leaving and I had known them for years. They were supposed to be my friends. I had done everything I knew to do. It wasn't good enough. I was a failure! I cratered. It was literally the lowest day of my life, or so it felt.

I was in a deep depression. Their words were like daggers to my soul. I did my best to try to convince myself it wasn't all my fault but it just felt like they were right. I believed it and I wanted to run. And I did!

I waited until they left. I canceled all of my appointments and I ran. Never in my life had I felt like a failure, but that day I did. It was horrible. I thought I had done the best I could but I was dealt a bad hand and it looked like the devil would win. I ran away. I drove up U.S. Route 287 to Wichita Falls. I drove all the way to my Mom's home. Tears coursed down my cheeks like a river. My heart was broken. All the years I had already given seemed to be empty. All my attempts to help and make forward progress seemed to have amounted to nothing. All I could think of was the rejection of the very people I had come to help.

Christ experienced that same rejection when He came to seek and to save that which was lost. He faced the rejection of mankind.

Perhaps you've been rejected by someone you love? You've done everything you can do. You've given and given. You've sacrificed and loved and yet you're ready to quit. Let me encourage you to hold on a little longer. A miracle could be just around the corner.

Even though I was 49 years old I felt like my life was over. I had nothing to live for... I was Pastor Failure! Dying would have been easy. Oh how I wished then I could have died.

Where Are You?

Later that night, my phone rang and it was my best

friend, my wife Danielle. "Where are you?" she said. I told her I was at my Mom's in Wichita Falls. In fact, I told her I was under the covers at her house in the guest room and wasn't coming out. I didn't want to talk to anyone. I told her that I was through and that I was going to quit. She said, "You're in Wichita Falls? That's six hours away... what happened?"

Thank God for an incredible wife. Thank God for people who won't let you quit! Who won't let you surrender! Who won't let you give up! Who won't give up on you. She began to tell me the other side. She began to build me up and tell me all the great things I had done... the hours... the days.... the years we had given to the ministry. When she said it, it sounded simple... when I thought about it, it sounded final! I was afraid, depressed and sinking deeper in despair.

Danielle has always had such a great way of putting things and that has been such a comfort to me. She's so good for me. She brings me down to earth. I needed her words. The person you're helping needs your words. They need your love. They need your understanding. Don't let them quit!

She Didn't Quit on Me!

Why as pastors do we worry over one or two grumblers and we forget about the many who love us? I'm so glad she's been my best friend… and what an anchor! That's what I've called her for years. The best thing she told me that night was, "Even if we go bankrupt and have no money to pay our own bills, if we have each other we will make it." When she said, "We will make it!" I realized she was in. And if we were broke who cares? If the Lord is with us, He won't let us go under… and if we do… we'll get to see how He'll bring us out on the other side."

"When you pass through the waters, I will be with you; and through the rivers, they shall not overwhelm you; when you walk through fire you shall not be burned, and the flame shall not consume you." (Isaiah 43:2 ESV)

That night was huge. She was in. She wasn't quitting. She was standing with me and we were not giving up. I couldn't say it for myself. I was so messed up. I needed someone to say it for me. For me, it was my wife. Thank God for a wife who stood with me and spoke those positive, healing words. It was exactly what I needed.

Through my experience of being healed, I saw how Christ has always carried my grief.

Medicinenet.com defines "grief" as the normal process of reacting to a loss. The loss may be physical (such as a death), social (such as divorce), or occupational (such as a job). Emotional reactions of grief can include anger, guilt, anxiety, sadness, and despair. Physical reactions of grief can include sleeping problems, changes in appetite, physical problems, or illness. I had all of them…

I needed emotional healing…
I needed Christ to touch me!
And I found…

Sometimes Christ carries my grief through others.
Sometimes Christ carries my grief through my wife.
Sometimes Christ carries my grief through a friend.
Sometimes Christ carries my grief through a healing word.
Sometimes Christ carries my grief through a time of prayer.
Sometimes Christ carries my grief through worship.
Sometimes Christ carries my grief through my family.
Sometimes Christ carries my grief through time.
Christ always carries my grief…
Christ always carries my sorrow…

Christ always carries my pain...
Christ always carries my difficulties...

"Surely He took up our pain and bore our suffering, yet we considered Him punished by God, stricken by Him, and afflicted. 5 But He was pierced for our transgressions, He was crushed for our iniquities; the punishment that brought us peace was on Him, and by His wounds we are healed. 6 We all, like sheep, have gone astray, each of us has turned to our own way; and the LORD has laid on Him the iniquity of us all."
(Isaiah 53:4-6 NIV)

Through His precious atonement and the sacrificial gift of Himself, I will forever be healed.

So many shared great words of faith with me. So many in the church encouraged me. On Sundays, I felt those saints all around me... but during the week, Satan climbed on my back and tried to talk me out of my victory. Words are powerful. A simple word can help heal you – or can catapult you into tragedy.

Words of Life!

Words are wonderful to us who enjoy their nectar. On my desk sits a coffee cup from my daughter. It was a gift for my 49th birthday. Written in her hand are the words "To the World you are one, but to one you are the world."

My children's words are so genuine and heartfelt. I love them so. Truly, we fail to realize how powerful words can be. How genuine your heart is when you say, "I love you." It's through those simple gestures of love and cheer that many helped carry me. Thank the Lord for little grandmas in the church who would hug me and tell me how awesome I was and "Keep the vision alive!" Whether it's a visit to a hospital room or walking by them at church… they know how to help you through the day. For most pastors it's like a drug. They make you feel invincible.

If you are your pastor's encourager… don't stop declaring the blessings of the Lord on his life. Bless him daily before the Lord. Through cards, letters, Facebook, social media (text or spoken), it is the best medicine for a broken heart. It's also a powerful preventative medicine. Encouraging words from you can counteract the dark, weary thoughts the devil puts in someone's mind… you're reminding them: they are worth loving; they are worth the life Christ gave so they could have life. The problem is that many times people need to hear the healing words that never come. Even if you feel like they may not need this or think you haven't even liked them up to now, go ahead anyway. Love them! Let your powerful healing words flow!

Some things just take time. It was Solomon who said, "For everything there is a season, and a time for every matter under heaven: 2 a time to be born, and a time to die; a time to plant, and a time to pluck up what is planted; 3 a time to kill, and a time to heal; a time to break down, and a time to build up; 4 a time to weep, and a time to laugh; a time to mourn, and a time to dance," (Ecclesiastes 3:1-4 ESV)

What Solomon was saying was that some things take time. This season will pass. If it's the season of breaking down, the season of building up will come. It's like the story of the guy who tried to help the caterpillar out of his cocoon. If you help by tearing away the membrane of the wrappings, the caterpillar will never become a butterfly. It needs the struggle. That process allows it to become what it is supposed to become. The best advice for the one reaching to help is give it time. This season will pass. A new season will dawn.

Chapter 4
He Carries Me Through...

God has lifted me through the difficult.

"When you pass through the waters, I will be with you; and through the rivers, they shall not overwhelm you; when you walk through fire you shall not be burned, and the flame shall not consume you."   (Isaiah 43:2 ESV)

"Surely He has borne our griefs, and carried our sorrows." (Isaiah 53:4a NKJV)

"The tongue has the power of life and death, and those who love it will eat its fruit." (Proverbs 18:21 NIV)

Discussion Questions

Have you ever grieved over your job, family, friends or finances?

What truth has the Lord revealed through your grief?

What or who have you turned to when faced with difficult times?

Family, Friends, Alcohol, Bible, Food... etc.

_____

_____

_____

_____

_____

Describe how the Lord has carried you.

1. _____
2. _____
3. _____
4. _____
5. _____
6. _____
7. _____
8. _____
9. _____
10. _____

"Victor Numquam Usque!"

Never Give Up!

Chapter 5
He Sometimes Removes

The summer of 2009 was hot and humid in Houston. The Great Recession was in full swing. Nothing was happening at the church property. We were the church without a home. We were meeting at a school, a former funeral home, and a day care center. In fact, I sometimes wondered if a big wind came up would it just blow us all away? We didn't need any more crises. We needed smooth sailing.

At the church property, work had been halted for months. Weeds were knee-deep growing everywhere. The yellow Tyvec siding had turned white in the bright Houston sunlight, waiting for bricks and stone to cover it over the passage of time.

It was a Tuesday. A few staff and I went to lunch together. It was our tradition to have our staff meeting and then go and enjoy lunch. We would conduct staff meeting in a small job site trailer, at the former funeral home, and then head out. Wow, those were tough times, but they were awesome times too! It was during those days, in the summer of 2009, that God started cutting away the Mike Allard who needed to die. Many days were dark but there were days of light also.

Nothing Changed!

Did I tell you it was hot? And nothing was happening? Like the old westerns where you'd see the buzzards circling overhead and a tumbleweed rolling by. Those buzzards were waiting for that guy to take his last drink. He's dusty and unshaven and he can barely walk. That's me. Finances were limited and lunch with the guys was actually a luxury. It was one of the few things I enjoyed. Forever, the church had always paid for that lunch. Now I was catching it. It was important. We needed it. We needed to relax and laugh. Little did we know how God was building our team. Someone once told me you build a team during tragedy or fun. Well, we had a whole lot of tragedy and we would always have fun at those lunches. Whether we were talking about the latest funny church story, sports or discussing the next sermon series... we had some fun times.

As was our custom, after lunch we dropped by the church property just to see it. I'm sure they wondered "Why are we going by there again?" Nothing had changed! There was nothing new! Week after week it just got more and more rundown. The walls were mildewed and covered in a layer of dirt. Trash blew across the parking lot. A few homeless people had come and left abruptly. On more than one occasion, a few stray dogs thought they had found a home.

It should have been finished by now, but it sat motionless. Weeds were growing up around God's vision. As we took a quick tour through the parking lot, in my green Ford F-150, there were a couple of old black crows sitting on the edge of the roof. Again, it was the perfect metaphor of the old western; two old buzzards sitting there staring at a carcass. Caw! Caw!

Stupid crows, I thought. Shut up! Go away! Caw! Caw!

Chance Abbott, our Assistant Master's Commission Director said, "Pastor, look at the crows, they're talking to you!" I think I said, "Hmm? Yeah...?" Nothing profound for sure.

Two Old Crows

He said, "Remember the story about the prophet Elijah and how the ravens came and fed him?" He said, "They're your birds!" My birds? Why are they my birds? I don't like crows! I thought to myself. "Uh" I said, "I see them hanging around here but I hadn't thought about it." Man, it was everything I could do to not be negative. I didn't want staff to hear me grumble but sometimes I couldn't help it. I was miserable. We are the embarrassment of churches and he's looking at birds! It's like, hey, we're drowning and you're looking at dumb old crows! I hate crows. There was nothing about them that I cared for. At the old church, crows picked at the rubber edging on the door seals. They're a bother. They're scavengers, they eat trash. They make noise. They destroy things. They bother me. Leave me alone crows. Go away!

Weeks passed and I would continue my journeys to the property. Every time I came, the crows were there. Walking around cawing. Talking and talking. Caw. Caw. Caw. Flying overhead screeching that annoying sound... Caw. Caw. The reality is that they were the only life at the church. No construction workers. No people... just two old black crows. Did I say I hate crows? I hate crows!

Days turned into weeks and I started remembering the words of my staff member: "They're your birds. Remember the prophet and how God used the ravens?"

Somewhere in those days, I started bringing them food. I would throw them an apple core and sometimes a stale donut. I'm not sure that's kosher crow food? They liked the donuts a lot more than the apple cores. They eventually became my companions. When I would go to the church property, I started looking for them. I think I even started talking to them. The hot Houston sun will do that to you. I would watch those crows. I drove up and thought about Elijah.

"And the word of the Lord came unto him, saying, 3 Get

thee hence, and turn thee eastward, and hide thyself by the brook Cherith, that is before Jordan. 4 And it shall be, that thou shalt drink of the brook; and I have commanded the ravens to feed thee there."
(1 Kings 17:2-4 KJV)

Elijah was on the run. He had had some amazing victories, but wicked Queen Jezebel was after him. Why is it that we can one day be God's great and mighty man of power and the next day we can sit in a corner worried about some old complaining saint? Elijah was hiding. If he had had caller ID, he wasn't answering.

My Hideout!

Where to hide? Sometimes we need to hide. Hiding is okay if you're hiding where God said to hide. I wanted to hide. I didn't want to see anyone and I didn't want them to see me. I didn't want to go to another meeting and think about how big a failure I was. No more church folks saying, "Pastor, when we gonna get in that building?" I just wanted to hide! In fact, if I could have gone to bed and not woken up that would've been all right too.

I remember playing hide-and-seek as a kid. You know how that works? You go hide while the guy who's "it" closes his eyes and counts to ten. You're looking for the perfect spot to hide. Is it in the closet? Is it under the bed? Or if it's outside – is it in the garage or behind a tree? Please hurry because he's already up to five and he'll open his eyes and come looking. "READY OR NOT, HERE I COME!" he yells.

Oh how I wanted to hide! It felt as though if God had counted to a billion that would have been okay with me... I was done. I was through with life. And little did I realize the hiding place He had for me. I think God knows us so well and prepares a special hiding place for each of us. A place that if we will look for it we can go there again and again.

His Hiding Place

In finding my hiding place I found Him! I found His hiding place for me. During those dark days I found that place. It's His hiding place! I sought Him and I found Him. The discovery of that place took time. It was a journey. Some would say it's a process. I think that's a good way to put it. Maybe even a quest! It's still the treasure in my morning. It's the first breath of life for me every day. I long for it. It's water to my soul. It's pure light shining in my dark space.

Unlike the childlike hide-and-seek game, where you run to find a place, Elijah was told where to hide. He was told to hide by the brook Cherith. It's always interesting to see if there is some deeper meaning with these places in the Bible. Cherith is one of those names from which we can draw some truth. It means "cutting; separation." Perhaps this brook was a place where the shepherd would separate or shear his sheep. For whatever reason Elijah finds himself at this place of cutting.

A Place of Cutting

It seems like crisis has a way of cutting away things. We get down to what is really important. We cut away the junk in our lives and start to do what is really necessary. Well, Elijah's place of separation or cutting was also a place of hiding. Sometimes God hides us to protect us. God needed some time to cut some things from Elijah. Perhaps he was cutting Elijah away from Elijah. Sometimes He hides us. Sometimes He separates us from the "stuff." He cuts away the things that we think are so important. He cuts away, and when He's through we sit there, remade and reshaped exactly as He wants us to be. The shepherd after cutting the sheep would apply salve or oil to the wounds. While cutting perhaps the sheep jumped or moved and more than wool got caught in the process. We've all been guilty of jumping and moving while we had something removed from our lives. We've grumbled and jerked as Christ patiently tried to remove the heaviness. We had grown the outer layer and it was weighing us down, sometimes unknown to us. Its weight was keeping us from moving freely. I had some things that needed to be cut away. There was a lot that I needed removed. Yes, there was some pride; arrogance; fear; jealousy; anger; and a lot of doubt.

A Dark Place

I was miserable. I wanted to hide. No, I wanted to die! I was at my brook Cherith. I had no more pride. I was filled with fear and doubt. My confidence was gone. This church had become such a burden. Pastoring wasn't fun. It wasn't a joy. I loathed my life and I sat in this dark place, but it was here I retreated. I would walk the moldy hallways praying "Oh God, Just let it all fall in on me!" Dying seemed like a better way out. That would have been easy! That would have been an answer to prayer.

I'm glad that sometimes God doesn't answer my prayers!

Oh, I'm sure there were a lot of lonely days down by that brook. There was no one else to talk to. There was nobody calling Elijah and asking him to come preach at their missions conference. Hey, Elijah come do a camp for us! Elijah, you're the man! No. Elijah was alone at the brook of cutting. He was sitting all alone at the brook and God was chiseling away. God was chopping away what wasn't needed. All alone. Yup, Elijah sat there day after day… night after night, all alone! Oh wait. No, there were the ravens that fed him. He had ravens (crows). They fed him. He wasn't alone…

Well, I started noticing those old crows. I remember a time when one got trapped in the common area of the front of the church building and couldn't get out. The building was still unfinished.

It was on one of my daily drive-bys… I was just checking on things. Coming into the tall foyer I heard him… man, was he making a racket! I had never been that close to a crow. He was huge. He cawed and cawed. I thought he would hurt himself banging into the windows. I thought he would hurt me! The room wasn't finished… debris was scattered everywhere and that old crow was just making a racket. I began opening all the glass doors along the front of the building. I was trying to give him the hint. This is the way out. Hey, buddy! You can get out this way. But I just had to wait for him to find it. I could only hope he would eventually get tired and see the opening and take it. Eventually he got tired and stopped flapping his wings. He landed, walked around, and realized there was a way out. It seemed like forever.

I had actually grown fond of those two old birds. No one else came out there. To keep vandals from walking away with everything, we paid people to sleep there. But as soon as morning came, they too would pack up and leave. So no one really loved to hang out there. I only did it because, well, it was my mess, and I had to figure out how to fix it. How silly I was!

You're Not Alone!

Once Elijah said, "Lord, I alone am the only one that is still around serving you!" The Lord, told Elijah, "'Lijah, now boy, there's 7,000 that haven't bowed their knees to Baal. Stop feeling sorry for yourself." (That was the Mike Allard translation.) Could it be that sometimes we just like to hear ourselves complain? I think if you look around you'll see you're not alone either. Neither was I. At that time there were a few hundred other people who were faithfully committed to following the Lord's vision. It just "felt" like I was alone. Just like it does for you.

That old crow flapped and flapped. He cawed and cawed. He made a bunch of racket. He was mad and wanted out of there. He wanted to fly but that building was just too small for his big wings to find flight.

Too many times we're like that. We're flapping around, banging into things, trying to get ourselves out of this mess. We're just making noise. When all the time... there's a door. We can escape. We just need to land and walk through it. We need to realize it's the door He's prepared.

Encouragement is a lot like that. Sometimes all you can do is show someone the direction of help... or the open door. You can only point them to a Scripture. You can only point them to the Savior. You can only share an encouragement and then… hope that they see it and take it.

Well, he saw it and when he did he took off. I watched him as he made his escape. He flew like crazy. He cawed back at me and cawed and cawed. I'm not sure what he said, but he didn't want anything more to do with being trapped. Fly, crow! Fly! And you know, he never got trapped in there again. I guess he learned a great lesson.

Somewhere in the process of seeking the Lord during my depression I decided to name those two old crows. I named them after the two prophets Elijah and Elisha. Day after day, I would come by the church and they were there. Many days, I've prayed and still pray around the church… and I hear those crows. I think back to when we weren't able to get that building finished. I think back to when I drove up one morning and said, in desperation, "God, we need a miracle! The offerings are terrible… finances are shot… no more reserves… what am I going to do? We're going to have to cut salaries. If we do who will quit first? And if they quit who will leave? GOD, we're not going to make it!" Sounds kinda crazy to think that you would speak to the creator of the universe like that? The one who made the sun, the stars, and all the planets. He's the one who sets the course of the oceans; He balances the air we breathe with proper consistency and flow. Yes, we were going under. We would probably not make it... so I thought, but I guess that's how we think.

When I drove up that morning it was like God was giving me this big old sign. At one corner of the building, standing like a sentinel at the roof, was one of those crows. At the other end was a sparrow and on the very peak of the roof was the other crow. They were each at their spots forming this beautiful triangle. It was as though God Himself had choreographed the scene. It was as if He was saying, "HEY, if I can take care of these old crows and this sparrow, I can take care of you!"

I CAN TAKE CARE OF YOU!

I heard it loud and clear. He was going to take care of me!

"Consider the ravens: for they neither sow nor reap; which neither have storehouse nor barn; and God feedeth them; how much more are ye better than the fowls?" (Luke 12:24 KJV)

A fella told me once, and I've never forgotten it, "I've never seen a skinny bird." Let that soak in... So if He can take care of the ravens (crows) and the sparrows, then guess what? He can take care of you. He knows exactly where we are. He knows what we need.

As I stood there alone by my brook Cherith... He would always be there. He would encourage me again and again! He would feed me meat every day.

My brook Cherith was the abandoned church building. It was dusty. It was moldy. It was deserted. But, it was where God met me every morning. I set up a chair and a small table and decided that every morning we would sit and fellowship together. Just the Lord and me. We would enjoy one another's presence. We still do, to this very day. So even though my situation didn't change immediately, my heart began to change. Out of the hurt and out of the storm came the greatest "finding-life-moment" of my life. I starting finding my life in that early morning prayer time. I started seeing I just might have a future, even if it was only the future of the next morning.

How can I encourage you, that He has not forgotten you?

Psalm 91 says, "He shall cover thee with His feathers, and under His wings shalt thou trust: His truth shall be thy shield and buckler. 5 Thou shalt not be afraid for the terror by night; nor for the arrow that flieth by day; 6 Nor for the pestilence that walketh in darkness; nor for the destruction that wasteth at noonday. 7 A thousand shall fall at thy side, and ten thousand at they right hand; but it shall not come nigh thee." Psalm 91:4-7 ASV

For me, many times I have heard those old crows caw, and I've thought if He can take care of them He can take care of me. I'm hidden in His secret place. I'm covered with His wings. He's my shield. I won't be afraid of the terror in the night. Thousands may fall around me... but it won't touch me.

For a long time it felt like I was just flapping my wings and banging into the windows wanting out. I wanted help; I wanted deliverance from the depression. How could I have gotten into this huge mess? Just like that old crow I didn't realize help had walked in.

You might just need to relax... rest... take a moment... Remember you're more valuable than a flock of old black crows and sparrows.

My Encouragers

Sometimes, I even thought those crows were talking to me. I guess it was the sun - it starts getting to you. Haha! They would caw caw. Maybe they were talking? Perhaps there's a crow that's been cawing overhead and you just haven't been listening. He's been trying to tell you, "Michael, Michael, The Lord is with you!" Believe me I had more than one precious saint tell me, "Don't give up." "You're God's man!" "This church is going to survive!" "Keep the vision alive!" Some of those old "crows" are worth listening to. And yes down at my brook of Cherith… they fed my soul. They fed my soul with love. They filled me with joy. They were a refreshing drink in a weary place. I started getting my joy back in pastoring because of the precious crows that fed my soul.

I've sat there at the brook of Cutting and Separation. Cutting and separation are never easy. Most of the time, we are oblivious to all that needs to be cut away. The rest of the time we realize there's something there but we're fidgeting so much, He can't do what He needs to do.

Lord, help me not to move while you chisel, while you work on me. Please, cut away what doesn't glorify you. Help me not complain and not cry too much. Help me hear the crows that are telling me how much you love me. Remind me of the secret place. The place you'll be waiting to see me. That place is worth all the things you have to move in my life. Get me to that place.

Help me to never give up!

Victor Numquam Usque!

Chapter 5
He Sometimes Removes

God has cut away some things in my life.

"And the word of the Lord came unto him, saying, 3 Get thee hence, and turn thee eastward, and hide thyself by the brook Cherith, that is before Jordan. 4 And it shall be, that thou shalt drink of the brook; and I have commanded the ravens to feed thee there."
(1 Kings 17:2-4 KJV)

"Consider the ravens: for they neither sow nor reap; which neither have storehouse nor barn; and God feedeth them; how much more are ye better than the fowls?"   (Luke 12:24 KJV)

Discussion Questions

What ways have you seen the Lord provide?
What things have you seen the Lord cut away from you?

What benefits did you find from the separation?

_____

_____

_____

_____

_____

Name some of the crows in your life.
Who are the people who've encouraged you?

1. _____

2. _____

3. _____

4. _____

5. _____

6. _____

7. _____

8. _____

9. _____

10. _____

Never Give Up!

Chapter 6

He Taught Me About Encouragement

I love a day off with nothing on the agenda, when the phone doesn't ring. I love it when no emergency situations are compelling me to respond immediately. I love a whole day just to enjoying only what I want to do. If that means rest, work in the yard, spending time in the garage, or just doing nothing… that's relaxing. I love it when Danielle is there but sometimes I just like being alone.

Then there are those other times when you wish the phone would ring or someone would text you or message you, but nothing… it's as though you're on Planet X and no one cares if you're alive or not… or at least that's the way it seems. Sometimes you want to be interrupted just so you know somebody was thinking about you.

There are times though when disaster comes and you find yourself feeling alone. You could be living the worst nightmare of your life and you wonder… will it ever end? You feel the loneliness of failure, or the loneliness of sickness, or the loneliness of divorce, or the loneliness of separation. It's like an army came and destroyed your world and now you're living in the ashes.

Ashes

David found himself in such a place when he came home, only to find the Amalekites had stolen every treasure he owned. What they didn't take they burned. Everything was ash! Destroyed! Ruined! His wives, his sons and daughters... all gone! Kidnapped! Life was supposed to be different. He was God's anointed. *How could this be? Lord, didn't you promise that I would be king? This doesn't feel like what I think a king should feel like. This feels horrible.*

The enemy had kidnapped his joy, kidnapped his precious family! Now what?

Who do you turn to? Who do you call, when life has stolen your peace? Not only was David robbed, but everyone else was too, and they were blaming David for their trouble.

A Turn in The Road

Ziklag was where David had been hiding out from Saul. It had been safe but now it was gone! The name Ziklag means "winding." I've often heard the saying, "A road is never so long that at some point it doesn't take a turn." One day it seems normal, and you're moving at a good pace. Things are going great, then there's a hill and a

114

turn and then another turn you didn't expect. Well, this was a turn David hadn't expected. How do you prepare for losing everything? I can't imagine the darkness of depression and fear that might have choked David's faith.

It's Your Fault

"And David was greatly distressed; for the people spake of stoning him, because the soul of all the people was grieved, every man for his sons and for his daughters: but David encouraged himself in the LORD his God."
(1 Samuel 30:6 KJV)

No one was running up to David saying, "Hey, it's going to be alright... we'll get them back... don't worry Davey... We're gonna make it... you just wait and see!"

No... everyone was blaming him. Failure! Loser! Why didn't you do a better job at leading? Aren't you God's anointed? If you were really a man of God, this wouldn't have happened to us.

Encouragement is defined as: "something that makes someone more determined, hopeful, or confident."

So, with no one there to encourage David, who does he turn to? No one to tell... not even some old crows... just himself.

What does he do? He encourages himself. He begins to make the Lord bigger than the problem. He retreats to the one thing that will secure his emotions. The Bible says, ...but David "encouraged himself in the Lord his God."

I love that little word "in." We view the whole thought without thinking of the power of that little preposition. I have found myself IN a lot of places, some of which I wished I had never seen. But, David goes INTO the secret chamber of the Most High. He runs to the shelter, the rock, the tower, the shield, the wall, the horn, the anchor of his soul – the Lord his God. It's not in his weakness that he goes to the Lord; it's his strength. This was why David was a success. He encouraged himself IN the Lord his God. He didn't wait for the phone call, or the email, or a buddy to drop him a note. We're not even sure how long it came for him to come to this conclusion, but we see David encouraged himself.

When you're at the bottom, sometimes you just don't hear kind words. You don't feel that anyone understands. You retreat when you should advance. You cower in front of the problem, when you should run to the Lord. You want to die. It's miserable to be that low. It's like falling in a hole, someone is throwing dirt in your face, and there is no way to escape. You want to give up. But David doesn't give up. He "encouraged himself in the Lord his God."

Why Didn't You Warn Me?

It took me a while to get there. I wanted to blame myself; and I wanted to blame God. I couldn't understand how He could let this happen. Where are you God? If I'm saved and praying as I should and living for you... why didn't you warn me? There isn't an easy answer to that...

It reminds me of Christ sending His disciples out in that boat one evening... and being the Son of God... He knows what's coming, right? A storm. Doesn't He?

In fact, it says, "Immediately Jesus made the disciples get into the boat and go on ahead of him to the other side, while He dismissed the crowd."
(Matthew 14:22 NIV)

He was fully aware of the situation. And He is always fully aware of where you are.

Somewhere in the middle of that sea a terrible storm hits. The waves were rolling; the wind was blowing; the disciples were rocking back and forth in that tiny wooden boat. Twelve men - bewildered and probably wondering what are we doing here? How did this happen? Didn't Jesus tell us to go to the other side? Yet here we are... alone... scared to death... wet... tired... weary... doing the Lord's work. Getting nowhere. It's strange how you can be right in the middle of God's perfect will and the whole world seems to be falling apart.

"...the wind was against it." (Matthew 14:24 NIV)

How can that be? Aren't we obeying when we go where Jesus wants us to go but the wind blows strongly against us? That can make for a strange turn of events.

I'm sure those disciples were baffled. Then it happened. Right out of nowhere, it gets worse... someone screams – a ghost! If life isn't bad enough why do things sometimes go downhill from the bottom of the hill?

This has to be the most terrifying moment, to be stricken with FEAR! The conversation in that boat had to have been on the edge. I'm sure there were not any thees and thous being spoken. There were no rhetorical cliches of "God is good, God knows right where we are..." The truth be told, there was probably a lot of screaming and yelling: "...grab that oar!" "Look out!" "Get us out of here!" "What...?" Maybe there were some words I can't even write.

It's sensational to say the least. No one is going to believe it, but Jesus does the truly impossible. He comes in the middle of the storm walking on the water to where they are.

118

He hasn't lost any of them. He knew exactly where to find them. He wasn't worried. But they were. Jesus never loses us. He knows exactly where we are. Most of all He knows the storm will never be forgotten, nor will they forget the powerful way Christ saved them. They'll remember for a lifetime that it wasn't their ability... it wasn't their decision... it was the mighty hand of God that brought them from that storm.

Go to Jesus

Ziklag, the Sea of Galilee, building a church, or a sickness with no end in sight but death... All of these things weaken us, but at the same time strengthen us. If we will just remember what Peter did. Go to Jesus. Get out of the boat. Go toward Christ. Do the impossible. Remember, He hasn't forgotten you. Thank God for the Apostle Peter. He asked the Lord, "If that is you Lord, bid me to come to you on the water." And Jesus always says, "Come!" Come to me all you who are burdened! Cast all your care on Him! Believe!

Peter is often remembered for his supposed failure on the water but he did get out of the boat. Eleven others stayed in the boat while He just wanted to be closer to the Lord! If I'm where He is... it'll be alright! I'll make it! If you'll just get close to the Lord, you'll make it also. He hasn't forgotten you.

It wasn't just me going through this, but key people around me were too. We were all feeling the sting of the economy and the delay of getting in the building. I found myself in a chasm. I thought several times of running, but where would I go... and it was so against everything I had preached. It was wrong to quit. The people who had placed confidence in me needed me to stand, to stand tall and not waver. We had left our old property... we were in mid-building of this new facility... and it was not going anywhere. Weeds and delays were the assault of the enemy. I didn't face Amalekites... no one had burned my church, and no one had kidnapped my family, but just like David, the comfort I found, I found IN the Lord!

And there were encouragers. The list is probably too many to count and I would hate to overlook any one person... so better to say, "Thank you! Thank you for your faith, for you words, for your love!"

A Crazy Idea

There was an earlier low season in my life. It was 2006 and I was trying to encourage myself. I felt so "out there" by myself. Leadership is just that a lot of the time. So I did something pretty strange. I needed some good news. I needed some encouragement. So I encouraged myself. I decided I would go on a fast and pray and I would write myself some letters. Yessir, write myself some letters. Every morning, I got up and wrote a letter. I filled my heart with prayer and Scriptures and then I wrote a letter. I wrote the letter as if I was in the church and somehow supernaturally God had spoken to me and was telling me to send the pastor a letter of encouragement. I knew exactly what he needed. It was a letter to the pastor. In fact, at one time I thought of naming this book just that: "Letters to a Pastor." Those were amazing letters. Faith was in every letter. Love filled the pages. They were from me and to me. I remember going to work that first morning and handing the letter to my secretary. She looked at me kinda puzzled. I asked her, "Would you mail that?" She saw it was from me and to me. She said, "Is this a joke?" I told her, "No, just mail it, please." She smiled and said, "Sure." It had to have seemed strange and it was strange, but it was awesome. Those letters started showing up every day. I looked forward to the mail. For seven days I wrote those letters. Seven powerful Holy Spirit-inspired letters came packed with Scriptures and encouraging words. It was like someone else was telling me, *Don't quit! Don't give up! You're gonna make it!* I wish I could say I still have those letters. When we moved from the old church they were packed away. I had kept them safe on a shelf in my old office but they were safely secure in a box to be opened when my new office was completed. Well, it was seven years before all those boxes were opened. I searched and searched but I've yet to discover where they went. One day, they'll show up. Those letters from the pastor to the pastor by the pastor about the pastor to encourage the pastor! Haha... what a story... but all true!

So if no one else will encourage you, encourage yourself in the Lord! Write yourself a letter.

To every encourager: keep encouraging! Keep praying; keep speaking; keep believing; keep reminding the soul you are helping. Maybe they are where I was. I would act as if things were fine and yet I was miserable. Instead of transparency I felt I needed to keep up a good front. That probably wasn't bad for the whole church, but around my friends I retreated. I could see on their faces they didn't know what to do either. What I really needed was a friend. Not to try and fix the problem, but someone who would just check on me and make sure I hadn't totally checked out. One or two did come by... but for the most part it wasn't until I began encouraging myself IN the Lord that real encouragement came.

Chapter 6
He Taught Me About Encouragement

When no one else could encourage me.

"And David was greatly distressed; for the people spake of stoning him, because the soul of all the people was grieved, every man for his sons and for his daughters: but David encouraged himself in the LORD his God."
(1 Samuel 30:6 KJV)

Discussion Questions

What do you do when you are discouraged: retreat, advance or run away?
Who has encouraged you?

What has the Lord taught you about encouragement?

_____
_____
_____
_____
_____
_____

Who do you know that needs encouragement?

Parents, Friends, Co-Worker, Teacher, Child… etc.

1. _____
2. _____
3. _____
4. _____
5. _____
6. _____
7. _____
8. _____
9. _____
10._____

"Letters to a Pastor"

Never Give Up!

Chapter 7
He Taught Me About Faith

Missions

The first Sunday of October 2009, I was at my lowest. That Sunday, a good friend of mine, Gary Sapp, was preaching at the school for me. It was a missions service and we were doing our best to keep that part of our church alive. Missions was a key to our turnaround. We had to get missions back as a priority. We had decided that even if we lose the church building, we can't stop missions!

We poured the foundation of the church on July 16, 2008, and then Hurricane Ike hit Houston in September. The Great Recession was beginning. For three weeks we couldn't have church at the school. It was terrible. We had moved away from the safety of the old Greens Bayou campus. That Sunday, after the hurricane, we had 12 people sitting on the doorstep of Summerwood Elementary. We tried using the school's outdoor pavilion but neighbors complained about the noise.

Those were trying times. Board meetings were tough. Offerings were small. But our source wasn't man and we were going through the fire. We had to get missions back as a priority, even with very little financial support.

We had gone through the worst year a church could face. As we honored God in missions, our finances turned. We had to step out and believe.

Faith Begins

That Sunday, Gary's message on missions was so profound. It was just the simple truth of what I hadn't done. Gary said, "Speak those things that are not as though they are! Stand in that place and declare what God says as though it's real!" It was a message of faith. It was a missions message I had preached myself, but now it was for me. It was about my faith. Where was it? How had I lost my faith? I was so worn down. I was so tired and exhausted from the daily grind of asking, "How will anything good come from all this misery?"

I really thought I was exercising faith by stepping out and doing this project; but had I really? James says, "Faith without works is dead." Well, mine was pretty dead. I needed life to come back into the picture. My faith was gone. I was on battery backup. It seemed as though everything that I tried up to this point had failed. As pastor, I truly was at my lowest point.

Declare the Unseen

I sat there and thought, "Wow, I've tried everything… I've run to every bank and lender I could find… I've done everything I could think of... yet one thing I hadn't... I hadn't stood in faith in that place and declared what wasn't as though it was. Jesus said, "You can speak to the mountain and it shall be moved." If He could move a mountain then I had an Everest that needed His attention. I needed it to move. If only it would move. What if it doesn't?

You might have a mountain just like that in your life. Perhaps it's a mountain of debt or a mountain of hurt.

I had preached to others but now I needed it. I needed it more than life. But the big question was what would happen if it didn't change? What would happen if I stood there and nothing took place? What if I actually went to the church and stood in that building and started declaring life? How long would I have to do that? What if I failed? What if it didn't work?

Why do we always think about prayer last? We had prayed but we had not declared life over the dead. That what wasn't *would* happen. Believe me I have found out there is a difference. Too many times we pray and excuse God from doing anything by our lack of declaration. We mix excuses in so we won't be embarrassed because what if? What if it doesn't happen?

A Journey of Faith

This last thing should have been my first thing. So before that sermon was over I had made my decision. I would begin a journey every morning. I would get up and go to that unfinished building and stand there and declare what was not as though it was.

That Monday, 5 a.m. came early. I woke up anxious to begin this new journey. I was throwing myself at the Lord's feet. So with a bottle of anointing oil and my Bible, I went to the church. It was dark and weeds were around the boards that formed the walkway. The main entrance steps were not finished and nor were the sidewalks. We had had just enough money to complete the foundation and most of the outer structure. Trash and weeds were there. Little mud holes and some lumber that had been used for form boards for concrete were there to walk on.

Only a single mercury vapor light hung buzzing in the sanctuary. The building was full of stuff. Sheetrock remnants, boxes, steel pieces of pipe for sprinkler systems, wire and piles of stuff everywhere. It was just a big shell with metal studs of future rooms. Empty doorways with no doors attached.

Anointing and Prayer

Every morning I would get up and head to the church. I Walked from doorway to doorway marking them with oil and prayer. Around the church I walked. I really don't remember how others found out I was there, but soon I was joined by one, then two, then three others. And that's the way it stayed for a while.

The first time I began to declare what wasn't there as though it was, it felt so strange. Listen, I believe in prayer and that God still answers prayer but what I was saying sounded strange.

I stood in that building and declared I see lights, walls finished, carpet on the floor, tile, and chairs. I see people filling this house! I hear the sound system, I see the projection system, I see the curtains and on and on I spoke. I tried to think of everything we needed and didn't have, all the little things. Each day, I would repeat the list but I would often think of something new. It was a different journey of faith. It was a real journey of faith.

"Now faith is the substance of things hoped for, the evidence of things not seen. 2 For by it the elders obtained a good report. 3 Through faith we understand that the worlds were framed by the word of God, so that things which are seen were not made of things which do appear." (Hebrews 11:1-3 KJV)

Framing My World

I remember it dawning on me one day, in prayer, that as I looked at that verse, "…<u>the worlds were framed by the word of God</u>…" I thought to myself, what world am I framing? Am I framing failure by all my negative talk? Am I destroying what God is trying to do with my lack of faith? I need to speak life into this vision. I had to speak faith. Never again would I say, "This will never happen!" From now on, I will speak life into this place of darkness and despair!

I stood there a long time, but I began to frame the world with God's word! I spoke those things that are not as though they were there…. "<u>…so that things which are seen were not made of things which do appear</u>."

"Death and life are in the power of the tongue, and those who love it will eat its fruits." (Proverbs 18:21 ESV)

Your words are important. What are you saying? Are you saying this will happen or are you saying it's impossible? Is life or death in your words?

"For verily I say unto you, That whosoever shall say unto this mountain, Be thou removed, and be thou cast into the sea; and shall not doubt in his heart, but shall believe that those things which he saith shall come to pass; he shall have whatsoever he saith." (Mark 11:23 KJV)

There is power in <u>YOUR</u> words. You can move the mountain or you can be under the mountain. What mountain are you creating? The mountain of doubt or the mountain of faith! With God all things are possible!

Agreement with Others

My first three prayer partners are unforgettable to me. One was a retired auto body man, Del Hines, who was one of my board members. There was also our future coffee shop guy, Brad Harlan, and a 65 year-old former sailor and welding instructor named Sharon Waszkiewicz. These were my three amigos. All three brought something special to the prayer meeting. I loved to hear Del pray! What a strong old voice. What an encourager. Pacing the building he brought this great cry of worship and Scripture. He was my Barnabas. He would spend his time quoting the word and crying out in intercession. Sometimes I would see him sit on an old golf cart we had in the sanctuary or he would simply kneel. Brad in his quiet way walked and prayed from room to room. Sharon was new to Crossroads and was very different. But different was good. We needed different. Wow, was she different! Sharon was a skater. Did I tell you she was 65 when this all started? She was very different in her prayer style. Sharon would skate the property every morning. She would skate seven times around the church and in all types of weather, every day. She was the mail carrier of prayer. Nothing kept her from her appointed rounds. Every morning speaking in tongues and with hands raised high, she would unashamedly declare outside what she believed would happen on the inside. She also skated down empty hallways and all through the building. In fact once (only once), I caught her skating on the flat part of the main roof. I drew a line there and said, "No, you're going to destroy the roof before I ever get us moved in." I still can't figure out how she climbed a 30-foot ladder wearing inline skates? I told you she was strange... but man did those three charge me up every day. Sometimes I remember coming to the church just because I knew they would be looking for me. I knew we were each other's accountability partners. We would not waver or quit on this prayer meeting. This was sacred. This was a divine appointment every morning, and the future and success of our church depended on our prayers. We were like four horsemen at the front of a battle. With sabers drawn we were charging the gates of hell. We were riding point on this spiritual battle every day.

Thank God for light moments of humor. I remember Sharon's first prayer meeting with us. She was new to Crossroads. Don't forget I said her military career was that of a sailor. We had called an all-day prayer meeting at the church. All through the day teams came to the unfinished building. This was back before we knew we couldn't complete the building. We were doing our capital campaign. All the teams had gone and I was the only one left. It was the close of the day with very few lights. We needed to be through by 7 p.m. It was getting dark.

I can still see that black Chrysler convertible coming through our back entrance and screeching its tires around the parking lot to where I was. At first, I thought what crazy person is this? Who is coming so late? You know sometimes you get frustrated as a pastor because nobody listens to announcements. Then again it could be trouble.

I got back out of the truck just in time to hear those brakes lock up. EEEEEEEK... Jumping out of her car she yelled, "Pastor, did I miss the prayer meeting?" I said, "Yes." Her immediate response was without hesitation, "Oh s***!" she exclaimed. "I can't believe I missed prayer meeting!"

I have to be honest. I've never heard that as a response to missing prayer meeting. It caught me so off-guard I had to laugh a little at the conjunction of prayer and her curse. I said, "Well, we can sure make a little more time for prayer. It sounds like maybe you might need a little bit of that." Thank God for the non-religious; the innocence of piety. Thank God for real people!

Yes, she was one of those precious gifts that God gave

me as I began ministering at the Crossroads. Raw, unadulterated faith! This was her church and she was determined to help her pastor get this building built. I'm not sure what I would have done if I hadn't had just simple loving people surrounding me every morning in prayer. We would walk the building. We would stop and sit somewhere. We would anoint walls and doorways. We would shout and speak in tongues! We would sing sometimes and pray and pray and pray! If there was anything that has marked my life, it was this journey of prayer. I still keep it to this very day. I love it! It's my journey to His secret place of refreshing me. Oh how I love Him and oh how I love those who journey with me. Many different ones have come and joined me...

The Conversation of Faith

Little did we know the bond that would come from those days of prayer. After our morning prayer meetings we would always gather together. Faith was the conversation in our unfinished future coffee shop. We would sit on camp canvas chairs and sit by heaters in the winter and fans in the summer. We would look out through the glass walls that were just keeping the wind away. We would stand in that place and declare the unseen as seen. I would say, "I see trees, and grass, and people driving in, and walking in, feeling the presence of the Lord!" We would try to imagine what it would be like when it was complete. We thought "What would be the next big thing God would do at the Crossroads?"

Living Faith

I had no idea of how amazing those days were. I had no idea of the man God was reshaping. Literally, they seemed like days where nothing was happening… but they were His days of drawing me close and sheltering me and protecting me and building my faith.

You see, if you never face anything and if you never go through trials, you'll never have faith. It'll never be precious. It'll never be pure. It'll never be costly.

Praying Faith

My early lessons of prayer and faith came from Pastor Granberry. "Michael, have you prayed today?" That has been Pastor Granberry's question for me for many years. When I was on staff as youth / children's pastor, he would ask me that question every day. "Michael, have you prayed today?" It was so common for him to ask it that if I hadn't made my way into the sanctuary to spend some time in prayer that morning, and I heard him drive up, well, I would immediately bow my head at my desk and utter a token prayer, just so when he asked me, I wasn't lying. "Yes sir, I've prayed today!"

I remember him asking me day after day. I've often wondered why me and no one else? Did he ever ask that question to others who worked for him? Many years later I asked him that question. What was it about me that he knew this guy needed to pray? I guess he could see that I needed it more than others. It was what changed me. This stubborn Texas boy needed some breaking and that "sweet hour of prayer" was just what I needed.

Even to this day, we laugh about it when we talk. He'll ask me on the phone, "Michael, have you prayed today?" "Yes sir, I have!"

I'm so glad I had someone who pushed me to be a man of prayer. What a great calling. As a pastor and man who leads people to a conversation with the Lord, I have to be. It brings the anointing. It breaks through the powers of darkness. It calls on the God of the Angel armies to come and fight in this battle for you. It's the game changer. It's what makes the difference in my day. It'll make the difference in yours.

"...we rejoice in our sufferings, knowing that suffering produces endurance, 4 and endurance produces character, and character produces hope, 5 and hope does not put us to shame, because God's love has been poured into our hearts through the Holy Spirit who has been given to us."   (Romans 5:3b-5 ESV)

"Draw near to God, and He will draw near to you. Cleanse your hands, you sinners, and purify your hearts, you double-minded." (James 4:8 ESV)

"Have you prayed today?"

Victor Numquam Usque!

Chapter 7
He Taught Me About Faith

What kind of world am I framing?

"Now faith is the substance of things hoped for, the evidence of things not seen. 2 For by it the elders obtained a good report. 3 Through faith we understand that the worlds were framed by the word of God, so that things which are seen were not made of things which do appear." (Hebrews 11:1-3 KJV)

"For verily I say unto you, That whosoever shall say unto this mountain, Be thou removed, and be thou cast into the sea; and shall not doubt in his heart, but shall believe that those things which he saith shall come to pass; he shall have whatsoever he saith."   (Mark 11:23 KJV)

Discussion Questions

What have you stopped praying about?
What kind of world are you framing?

Do you pray specifically <u>for</u> or <u>against</u> things?

Sickness, Sin, Deliverance, Power, Help... etc.

_____

_____

How has faith changed your life?

Direction, Attitude, Heart... etc.

1. _____
2. _____
3. _____
4. _____
5. _____
6. _____
7. _____
8. _____
9. _____
10. _____

Never Give Up!

Chapter 8
He Will Fight For Me

During the struggles we faced in 2009, I started a new sermon series entitled *Victorious Secrets.* It featured Victory Secrets every believer needs to know. However, at the time, I felt no victory. For nine months we had had no activity on the building of the church. It was growing four-foot weeds and because of vandals we were paying people to watch it at night. Nothing was on the horizon except bad news. We were barely holding our own. In fact, I didn't have an ounce of victory in me… or at least that's what I "felt." But faith doesn't walk by feeling; faith walks by the truth of God's word.

The Struggle

Why does God give me messages that have everything to do with what I don't have and everything I need? Maybe I'm the only preacher who's preached a sermon out of my lack. I was going to be a bad example of this topic. But, looking back, it was exactly what we needed as a church. We were at an all-time low. Coming out of the summer we needed some miracles - we needed victory. It was truly a challenge for me to deliver this… God was instructing me to tell the people to see the unseen!

"Now the king of Aram was at war with Israel. After conferring with his officers, he said, "I will set up my camp in such and such a place." 9 The man of God sent word to the king of Israel: "Beware of passing that place, because the Arameans are going down there." 10 So the king of Israel checked on the place indicated by the man of God. Time and again Elisha warned the king, so that he was on his guard in such places. 11 This enraged the king of Aram. He summoned his officers and demanded of them, "Will you not tell me which of us is on the side of the king of Israel?" 12 "None of us, my lord the king," said one of his officers, "but Elisha, the prophet who is in Israel, tells the king of Israel the very words you speak in your bedroom." 13 "Go, find out where he is," the king ordered, "so I can send men and capture him." The report came back: "He is in Dothan." 14 Then he sent horses and chariots and a strong force there. They went by night and surrounded the city. 15 When the servant of the man of God got up and went out early the next morning, an army with horses and chariots had surrounded the city. "Oh, my lord, what shall we do?" the servant asked. 16 "Don't be afraid," the prophet answered. "Those who are with us are more than those who are with them." 17 And Elisha prayed, <u>"O LORD, open his eyes so he may see."</u> Then the LORD opened the servant's eyes, and he looked and saw the hills full of horses and chariots of fire all around Elisha."
(II Kings 6:8-17 NIV)

Victorious Secrets

There's definitely a victorious secret here! It's the secret of the unseen. In the world of faith and challenge, victory is first, always unseen. Because it's unseen, fear might remain. We fear what we see. We see the doctor's report. We see the empty house after a spouse leaves. We see rejection and anger from a teenager, living in rebellion. We see the notice of being fired from a job. We see our problems like an enemy invader landing on the beaches of our life.

Outnumbered

Elisha's servant didn't see what Elisha saw. He saw the army surrounding them. Elisha saw victory! Elisha saw the unseen as seen! Elisha realized God's army was there and that the enemy was outnumbered.

"'O LORD, open his eyes so he may see." Then the LORD opened the servant's eyes, and he looked and saw the hills full of horses and chariots of fire all around Elisha."
(II Kings 6:17 NIV)

I had to begin seeing my church as Christ saw it. Not incomplete. Not in shambles and covered in mold and weeds. But I had to see it as He saw it. Complete with everything. It's the secret of the unseen. I had to stand in that church building physically and declare the unseen as seen. That's faith.

Stand and See

That's standing at the Red Sea, seeing the crashing of the waves; hearing the sea gulls and yet believing for a path through the middle on dry ground. You don't *practice* that faith - you *live* that faith.

That's standing on the battlefield seeing the giant defeated. It's lying down in the lion's den and going to sleep. It's pressing through a crowd, knowing the moment you touch Christ you will be healed. That's seeing the unseen.

Fear separates us from what God's truth tells us is there. Fear tells me it won't happen. Fear tells me it's impossible. Faith tells me with God all things are possible.

One of the things I've often told the church was, "We weren't supposed to make it. We're here because The Lord helped us." the Lord is constantly working in the unseen to reveal it to be seen through our faith.

Impala Faith

African impalas can jump to a height of over ten feet and

at a jump cover a distance of greater than 30 feet. Yet these magnificent creatures can be kept in an enclosure in any zoo with a three-foot wall. The animals will not jump if they cannot see where their feet will fall. Faith is the ability to trust what we cannot see... to jump and not know how the landing will end... but knowing that the Lord will be there when you land.

It's not only the fear of what I see that separates me from God's future for me, but also the fear of what I hear. So ask yourself, "What am I allowing myself to hear? Is it causing fear or faith to rise?

"So faith comes from hearing, and hearing through the word of Christ." (Romans 10:17 ESV)

Are the voices around you speaking words of faith or words of fear? With what are you allowing your mind to fill up? Victory is not always heard immediately. Victory is first heard through words of faith.

My No Faith Promise

I sat in another missions service several years later, and the speaker challenged us to step out by faith. I wrote down "My Faith Promise," or "My <u>Know</u> Promise" (what I knew our church could do – my "I know we can do this" promise); better yet, "My <u>No</u> Promise," (which really wasn't a faith promise it was MY NO FAITH PROMISE).

I was only willing to do <u>something I knew we could do as a church</u>. Remember, giving to missions was a big turnaround for our church. When things got financially difficult, we looked for a new missions project to support. It's become one of our great core values. It's a Victory secret.

Faith is seeing the impossible as possible. Faith is the dream. Faith is your God promise. Faith is when God has to help you to reach it. <u>Where is the faith if you do what you know you are able to do</u>? At that moment, the Holy Spirit convicted me of my lack of faith! Why had I believed for so little? I was proud of the commitment. It wasn't anything to sneeze at. It was a $25,000 commitment! But we had done that the year before, so where was my faith for this year? Where was the stretching for the future?

Works of Faith

With conviction, the Holy Spirit doubled that amount in my heart. At first, it seemed more than we could do. Then He dropped this truth in my heart. <u>It will never happen until you have written it... prayed it... and declared it...</u> It's part of the works of faith James said. "Faith without works is dead." Begin living it like it's real. Write it down! Say it out loud! Believe it! Declare it! I had never thought of it like that. I had to believe it! I had to write it down, say it out loud, believe it and declare it done! That's faith! Too many times we are scared to say things we believe in our heart. If it never comes out it will always sit dormant. Faith needs to be spoken. Faith needs to be thrown into the light of day and declared. The woman with the issue of blood had to venture out of her home. She had to get out of that sick bed and find her way to the Master. Jesus asked the question: "Who touched me?" Don't you think He already knew the answer?

"For everyone born of God overcomes the world. This is the victory that has overcome the world, even our faith. 5 Who is it that overcomes the world? Only he who believes that Jesus is the Son of God."
(1 John 5:4-5 NIV)

So victory is a faith that believes Jesus is the Son of God. He is the Lord over my situation. Victory is not always seen, nor is it always heard, and very rarely is it felt, before it is seen. I didn't feel like things would change but I couldn't be moved by what I felt.

You may not feel better the moment you pray for healing, but that doesn't mean you're not healed. Christ purchased that healing with His life, with His body, beaten and broken for you! We declare the unseen as though it is real!

We ask people, "Well, how do you feel about that?" The

truth is, it really doesn't matter how we feel about it. It's what does God's word say about it, and then what am I doing about it? I can't tell you how many times I haven't felt victorious but victory was already there.

Victory Celebrated

Our victory was won at the cross and celebrated at the tomb! At the cross it seemed defeat was all that could be seen. The blood, the gruesome death, the nails, the discarded garments, the tears from a grieving mother, the hollow faces of disciples trying to make sense of what had happened. Victory seemed a million miles away, but victory was more alive that day than on any other day in history. His precious blood had been sacrificed and was at that moment being spread upon the mercy seat of heaven. His anthem of worship was being sung by the angels. The unseen were rejoicing over the seen. And when the morning of the third day arrived, it was from a tomb with soldiers on guard that He arose from the dead. One minute it looked like defeat and decay. Then suddenly, an earthquake, angels, a gravestone rolling; victory that was unseen was now seen! Little did those disciples realize the noise of defeat of the nails being hammered was actually the sound of victory! Little did they realize that life would come forth from that grave.

Life will come forth from your grave! Wait for that dawn.

The dawn of that powerful realization that He has not forsaken you. He hasn't left you as an orphan, but He has come to set you free. And that freedom is real and it is present. It's time to walk in the liberty for which Christ has set you free!

Close the Gates

In the old city of Jerusalem there are many different gates: the Damascus Gate, the Dung Gate, the Lion's Gate, and so on. Well, just as these ancient cities had different gates we have gateways into our lives. We have the eye gate; the ear gate; the touch/feeling gate and the emotion gate. These are those sensory areas by which we live. We are protected by them. We understand fire and cold by these senses. Gates allow things to come in and out. With faith you have to close those gates and believe. Too many times my eyes see things that cause doubt. My ears hear bad reports and fearful words. My emotions may fill up with depression and despair. So… I have to close those gates and let the walls of faith surround me. Surround yourself with His word! The Psalmist said it like this…

"**You are a hiding place for me;** you preserve me from trouble; you surround me with shouts of deliverance. Selah" (Psalm 32:7 ESV)

Think about the doctor who gives a vaccine or an

injection of medicine. You need a faith injection. You need to be inoculated from fear/doubt/depression and anxiety. We are vaccinated with faith when we believe on Christ as Savior. You may have never seen a miracle but that doesn't mean miracles don't happen. You just haven't seen it yet. Don't stop asking, don't stop believing... Never give up! "Numquam Usque!"

Pastor and author Francis Frangipane said it like this... "Instead of praying for victory, we settle for temporary relief. We pray that God will make the devil leave us alone, when the Lord is telling us to pursue our enemies and scatter them like dust."

Get Sick and Tired

When I was a kid, mom used to make my brother and me draw an imaginary line between us in the back seat. It would work for a few minutes but we would always see who would push the line and eventually we were fighting again. Stop trying to draw an imaginary line between you and the devil. He will lie and tell you he'll leave you alone. His goal is very real. My brother and I were typical siblings. We fought often and we fought to win. When we were young he picked on me. I would cry and here would come momma to break it up. Eventually it got to the point I was tired of him hitting on me and hitting on me. I remember the night I hit him square in the face for the first time. I was shocked! I had hit him with such force that he fell to the ground. It felt so good. I was tired of the picking. I was tired of the taunts and just as I got tired of my brother's picking… you've got to get sick and tired of the devil. You've got to square your stance and go to battle. Realize you are a victorious child of God. He's called you to be the head and not the tail. He calls you more than a conqueror. It's time to hit the devil square in his face. Fight back… don't take "no" for an answer. And never quit believing!

"The Lord will fight for you, and you shall hold your peace." (Exodus 14:14)

"Be still, and know that I am God; I will be exalted among the nations, I will be exalted in the earth! 11 The LORD of hosts is with us; The God of Jacob is our refuge." (Psalms 46:10-11 NKJV)

When Israel first stepped foot into the Promised Land, it was a battle. When you first step foot in the path to follow the Lord… you are taking territory that the Lord has already won. Remember, Satan doesn't want to give up that territory. You may sense you are up against something new. You are a new creation and you are breaking free. It's a new step for you but it's a place He has already given to you.

Spiritual Jericho!

There are promises, like a spiritual Jericho, that are yours. You just have to walk in obedience and follow what He says for you to do. For Israel it was a new voice, a shout of victory! They needed to rejoice over what God had given them before they received it. That first conflict, at Jericho, was unseen and unheard until Israel shouted! To the natural person it might have seemed foolish. The strategy was simple and it was clear... shout on command!

"Now Joshua had commanded the people, saying, 'You shall not shout or make any noise with your voice, nor shall a word proceed out of your mouth, until the day I say to you, 'Shout!' Then you shall shout."
(Joshua 6:10 NKJV)

Joshua realized that the words of our mouths either build up our faith or build up our doubt. So until he said, "Shout!" they were to remain silent. It's like momma always said, "If you can't say anything good, don't say anything at all." Let's turn that around. If you can't speak words of faith it's better to be silent.

It's easy to start complaining and feel sorry for yourself. It's also easy to allow anxiety to fill our conversations. Joshua realized this and so silence was the order. Not until that week was over and on the seventh day on the seventh trip around the walls of Jericho with horns of the priest blasting and with the crunch of marching feet being the only sound did Joshua command, "Shout, for the Lord has given you the city!" Then, before the walls started crumbling, they shouted! At that moment there was nothing to shout about, only because the command was given. Not until they had <u>obeyed</u> the command and shouted… did the walls begin to move!

How many times have you stood by faith and prayed? In the seen world, nothing seemed to be happening, but in the unseen it is beginning.

It's that moment when you have prayed it, declared it, believed by faith, that God creates it in heaven so that it will be formed in this world. Just believe, and ask not wavering and see what happens!

"Assuredly, I say to you, whatever you bind on earth will be bound in heaven, and whatever you loose on earth will be loosed in heaven." (Matthew 18:18 NKJV)

Change the Conversation

He will fight for you. He hasn't forgotten you. Begin to change your conversation. Stop repeating the lies you hear the enemy speak, but speak those words of faith. Speak what God's word says. You're not asking this for your empty wants but for the miracle that's got to happen.

For me I had to make it an appointment. Every day I would pray that list of faith. If you can't say it out loud then write it down. The truth is a doctor will tell you something and you will repeat it to everyone you know. He's just a man. He might have several degrees, but the ruler of the universe, the God of all heaven, has a different report for you.

I remember a young couple faced such a day. I received word that Louis and Julie Aguirre's little twin daughter Rihanna was not expected to make it. She had contracted spinal meningitis. The doctors, while trying to help her, had caused several mishaps in her treatment. Her heart had stopped and they had revived her. It was horrible. It was a parent's worst nightmare. They were crushed.

I had known this family from back in the day at the old church. Louis was one of our musicians. He had made it out to some of our early prayer meetings. His work schedule kept him from being there all the time. They were a precious young couple with a beautiful set of twin girls. Everything wonderful was in their future. These are the tough moments in being a pastor. Helping a family during tragedy.

It was in a cold conference room at Texas Children's Hospital that we met. I had been in on meetings like this before. Many times it's been my part to sit with a family when doctors have to tell a family some terrible news. It's so vivid in my memory even to this day. Seven specialists walked in wearing their white doctor's coats with grim faces and they began to tell Louis and Julie the worst news. They said things like, "Your daughter will probably not make it. If she does she may never speak, walk, or develop like her sister." The worst thing they said was, "The gray matter has probably already been destroyed." Their description was so cold and matter-of-fact. I know they had to do their jobs but it was very sterile. My heart was broken for them. My mind raced ahead as I thought what they were saying is that she's going to die, and if she lives her brain will be so affected she will be an invalid. Tears filled our eyes.

There wasn't an ounce of promise coming from those doctors and they were "the specialists." Not a thread of hope. Nothing! Not even "We will wait and see what happens." They had all made up their minds that she was not going to make it and if she did, she would be a cripple for life.

A Holy NO/KNOW!

I remember Elva, Louis' mom was there also, and the four of us walked out and slowly walked to that little girl's hospital room. None of us agreed with what the doctors had said. "No, we don't accept this. This is not how it's going to be." As we walked into her room you could hear the typical sounds of beeping and breathing sounds. Her tiny little body was made comfortable by towels and cushions around her, but there was no comfort in that room. Until...

It wasn't until we began to pray and speak what we knew was the truth of God's word. It wasn't a room filled with NO FAITH. It became a room of KNOW FAITH! Somewhere, in the middle of that prayer the powerful presence of our risen Savior Jesus Christ walked into that room. Our prayers began to rise above the room right into the presence of God. I remember saying, "She will live and she will be healthy and she will excel in everything, and in fact she will even excel above her sister." Why I said that I don't know, other than I was mad. I was mad at the devil. His deception with Adam had caused all of this. He is a liar and the father of all lies. There is no truth in him.

How dare they not give this family a thread of hope? As we prayed, our words weren't pleading words. They were words of declaration. They were words of faith. We didn't scream. It wasn't a room filled with loud voices, just voices declaring what wasn't as though it was.

Rihanna will be healed. She is going to walk. She is going to talk. She will run. She will live. She will excel above her sister. She is going to live!

You know I left that day knowing I had felt the presence of the Lord in that hospital room.

I remember getting the call. Just 24 hours later the doctors were saying, "It seems she's taken a turn for the better. It looks like we might have been wrong." Sure enough little Rihanna did get better and she did recover completely. In fact, I see her every week at the Crossroads. Her and her sister can't be missed. They are two of the most beautiful little twins. Oh, and Rihanna is taller. She's above her sister. Haha… The Lord hears every detail in our prayers and He answers them. So begin to declare the unseen as seen.

Write it down!
Believe it!
Declare it!
Shout it!

The Aguirre family – Louis, Julie and the twins, Rachel and Rihanna. Can you guess which one is Rihanna? She's the one on the right… the taller twin! It's been seven years since her healing.

Victor Numquam Usque!

Chapter 8
He Will Fight For Me

I've already won because He won!

"For everyone born of God overcomes the world. This is the victory that has overcome the world, even our faith. 5 Who is it that overcomes the world? Only he who believes that Jesus is the Son of God."
(1 John 5:4-5 NIV)

"You are a hiding place for me; you preserve me from trouble; you surround me with shouts of deliverance. Selah" (Psalm 32:7 ESV)

"The Lord will fight for you, and you shall hold your peace." (Exodus 14:14)

Discussion Questions

Have you ever lost a fight?
Has anyone ever fought for you?
How did that make you feel?

How Has the Lord Fought For You?

_____
_____
_____

_____

_____

Who could you fight for in faith?

1. _____
2. _____
3. _____
4. _____
5. _____
6. _____
7. _____
8. _____
9. _____
10. _____

Faith!

Never Give Up!

Chapter 9
He Just Needs One

"And I sought for a man among them, that should make up the hedge, and stand in the gap before me for the land, that I should not destroy it: But I found none." (Ezekiel 22:30 KJV)

In Ezekiel's time God was looking for a man. He was looking for one person to stand in the gap. He was looking for one person to be a game changer.

I've seen God use one person to change everything. Sometimes it's that person who calls you in the middle of the day and says, "Pastor, you're doing a great job!" Or the one who drops a note of encouragement in the mail. It's the new convert who looks at you and says, "Now what, Pastor?" Over and over, one willing, serving heart has changed the course of everything. For me, one of my greatest game changers was a wrecker driver. His name was Herb. I was a new children's and youth pastor at the church and I had a lofty vision for what I was hoping God would do with my part of the church.

"But Jesus looked at them and said, "With man this is impossible, but with God all things are possible." (Matthew 19:26 ESV)

Herb

I remember the first day I met Herb Thayer. It was back in the early '80s and Danielle and I were the youth/children's pastors at the old church. It was a Sunday morning, and our children's service was in full swing. This mammoth man with greased-back black hair, Terminator sunglasses, and a cell phone the size of a Kleenex box, came walking into our children's service. You would expect the soundtrack from *Mad Max Beyond Thunderdome* to be playing in the background - or perhaps *Born to be Wild!* He was a BIG man. He boasted later that when he was younger he had been a bodybuilder with Arnold Schwarzenegger! He was now far removed from those days, but he was definitely big, and definitely strong. As big as he was, we soon found that his heart was bigger.

There was one thing for sure about Herb - he loved his family. His wife and three daughters were his treasures. When he found Jesus, he wouldn't settle for anything less than all of them attending church, every time the doors were open.

When I first met Herb, he and his wife Becky had only two little girls. They were the joy of their lives. They came to children's church with their beautiful little dresses, church shoes and purses. We soon found out that Herb and Becky always made sure that their daughter Melissa had a $25 check in her purse, every week, for the offering contest. Then later, when their daughter Michelle started attending she had the same.

Herb was my fan and my friend. He was a gift from God. It helps so much, when you're in the ministry, to have that one person who believes in you! Who believes you can make it! Herb believed in me and my vision. Whatever he heard come from my mouth, Herb wanted to make it happen. He was a king! He loved me because I loved his kids. As ministers of the gospel we have to be careful with people like Herb because they are easy to use to your own advantage when it's a whim and not a need.

I remember that God had laid on my heart the desire for a thriving bus ministry. Herb wanted to help make that happen. I placed a bus on the pulpit one night and simply said I felt God was going to help my little bus grow. Well, that next week, a boy from our youth group called and said his dad had a bus. The bus ran well but was just sitting dormant in their back alley. He had wanted to make it into a motor home of sorts but never had. Dad was drunk and asked his son, "What should we do with that bus?" The boy said, "Brother Mike is trying to start a bus ministry, so why don't we give it to him?" Before he could sober up, Danielle and I went over there, and I drove that bus to the church that night. It was kinda funny - on the side of the bus was this

Victor Numquam Usque!

message, "My little dog house." That night, I thought, "I hope I'm not gonna be in the dog house with Pastor Granberry when he sees this bus in the parking lot tomorrow!"

Pray it in!

I had asked Brother Granberry if I could have a bus ministry and he had said, yes, but the church didn't have the money. He told me, "You'll have to pray it in." Well, that's what I had been doing and now we had our first bus.

Too many times we don't exercise faith. I wouldn't take anything for those early days of faith. Pastor Granberry taught me to pray things in. He taught me to stretch my faith and believe. That if God gave it, God would provide. Don't make it easy on your staff. If we haven't first prayed over the ministry and its needs, we have missed our greatest resource. What I learned through those early days of praying it in was critical to the successes later that I've had in praying it in. If God can provide the $1,000 today, God can provide the $1 million tomorrow! We just have to pray it in!

Then I heard about four buses in Wichita Falls. That's where Herb came in; he asked me if he could help! All four buses would be auctioned off and I hoped to buy a few of them. They all sold for $3,600. We bought them

172

all with Herb's help. Now understand, Herb wasn't a wealthy man by any means, but he was one of our greatest givers at the church. As a wrecker driver, he would run that truck all night to pay an extra missions commitment. That's the power of one. One person who wants to can make a huge difference. Herb gave the money. He stood in the gap...

"Carry each other's burdens, and in this way you will fulfill the law of Christ." (Galatians 6:2 NIV)

Now I had five buses but I didn't need all five at one time. A man in my church, responsible for relocating a lot of workers with Brown & Root, worked at different job sites. He came to me and asked me if he could rent a couple of those buses for a few months. This had never dawned on me. Not only did I have my bus ministry but it was now making money. It was putting money back into the ministry. I still can't believe we rented two of those $800 buses for seven months for $1,000 a month. That was $7,000 I needed to run that ministry. Then he turned around and bought those two buses from me for $3,500. In just seven months God had supplied over $14,000 to this little children's pastor. I had only prayed... and God had provided this supernatural provision by using three very unlikely people.

Through the years Herb Thayer was a wonderful friend. He was a wonderful man of God. He wasn't perfect and usually at every altar call, he was the first to go forward. He was an awesome man and showed me the power of one. One person can become a big game changer for your future. He stood in the gap and made up the hedge.

The Lord is Searching for One!

"For the eyes of the LORD run to and fro throughout the whole earth, to show Himself strong on behalf of those whose heart is loyal to Him..."
(2 Chronicles 16:9 NKJV)

The Lord is searching for that one person! David was one. The giant Goliath challenged Israel... "Send me out a champion!" David wasn't a warrior. He was only a shepherd boy. Not your typical SEAL Team Six fighter. But he was one. One who believed that the Lord would help him defeat this enemy. Saul needed one warrior. All through his army not one came forward to fight. A simple little shepherd boy was the one. Don't underestimate the one sitting in your congregation. Don't underestimate what God will do with the power of your one faith promise. It's not the mighty and it's not the biggest giver that usually makes the difference. It's the one with the greatest faith that truly turns the tide.

Daniel was one who refused to bow to new laws and demands of compromise. He was one who was willing to face the den of lions to prove his God is faithful.

The Lord is searching for one! One person to step out of the crowd. Esther was one such person. When all of God's people would be destroyed Esther stepped from the shadows and became one God could use. For such a time as this she was the one.

Joseph was one who stood in the gap also. He was one who dreamed a dream and believed God for that dream. He didn't know how it would happen, but he knew God had given him the dream. You may not understand all that God is going to do through you, or when He will do it, but you can rest assured, if God gave you that dream, it will happen.

What do you do when you feel you don't even have one person? Well, remember you have the Lord. He believes in you and is standing with you. Paul said to the Corinthians…

"…thanks be to God! He gives us the victory through our Lord Jesus Christ." (1 Corinthians 15:57 NIV)

So stop doubting God's promises! Look at the supernatural provision and promises He's given to you. Wait on Him. Be that one who stands in the gap and makes up the hedge.

Be that one who encourages your pastor. Be the spouse who encourages your husband or wife that they are going to make it. Be the one who talks them out from under the covers of depression. Be the one who reminds friends they are not forsaken and they will make it! The Lord is on their side! Your words are words of healing.

Your words are words of faith that they need to hear!

Chapter 9
He Just Needs One

**God doesn't have to have a crowd,
He just needs one.**

"And I sought for a man among them, that should make up the hedge, and stand in the gap before me for the land, that I should not destroy it: But I found none." (Ezekiel 22:30 KJV)

"But Jesus looked at them and said, "With man this is impossible, but with God all things are possible." (Matthew 19:26 ESV)

"...thanks be to God! He gives us the victory through our Lord Jesus Christ." (1 Corinthians 15:57 NIV)

Discussion Questions

Have you seen one person make a difference?

What keeps you from being that person?

_____

_____

_____

_____

_____

_____

_____

Who do you know for which you might be their one?

1. _____
2. _____
3. _____
4. _____
5. _____
6. _____
7. _____
8. _____
9. _____
10. _____

"Will You Be the One?"

Never Give Up!

Chapter 10
He Taught Me About the Impossible

Sometimes the greatest conflict is the conflict going on inside of you. It's the conflict of the mind. It's the battle that rages between faith and fear. It's the question that walks up to the castle of your faith and throws flaming missiles at your future. As believers we are too many times hiding in that castle praying the devil will leave us alone instead of charging the fear and challenging it with the Word of God!

Living in Conflict

The phone rang in the tiny job site trailer we used for an office, and my secretary told me, "There's a man on the phone who wants to give us grass!" I responded with a negative tone, "Nobody wants to give us anything... nobody wants to give us grass... I'm sure he's just wanting to sell us something. Nobody wants to give us anything!" As negative as I could be, that's how it sounded! I was jaded and negative. On one hand, at prayer, I was God's man of faith and power, but in the real world I was as negative as a person could be.

I was waking up and coming to the Lord's house praying and believing by faith. I was speaking words of faith over this vision. It sounded good when I prayed it but it wasn't what I was living.

Too many times, what we say in prayer is completely different than what we say in real life. When the fever is high and the temperature is rising we scramble for doctors and medicine and pass over the oil and prayer. We've been given the greatest tools of faith and they sit on the shelf.

"Is anyone among you sick? Let him call for the elders of the church, and let them pray over him, anointing him with oil in the name of the Lord. 15 And the prayer of faith will save the one who is sick, and the Lord will raise him up. And if he has committed sins, he will be forgiven. 16 Therefore, confess your sins to one another and pray for one another, that you may be healed. The prayer of a righteous person has great power as it is working." (James 5:14-16 ESV)

I told my secretary, "Why don't you have one of the Board members call him and see what he wants?" Truthfully, I didn't want to waste my time on some salesman driving by seeing we needed grass and trying to sell me some grass! Grass?! We didn't need grass! We needed everything! The church was a mess! The outside Tyvec was bleached white. The stone work and the brick work were unfinished. The sidewalks and entries to the building were not completed. The place was just full of items. We had stored future church furniture and stuff for the move into the new building in outside storages. Then, when it became apparent we weren't moving in, we moved it in to store it in the building... until it was completed. We didn't need grass... We needed cash!

At one time when I was at my lowest, I yelled at one of the finance group representatives (the group who left us), during a phone conversation. I said, "If we go under I'll spray paint the name of your organization on the front doors of this building, with your phone number, and write in giant letters that you screwed us!" Wow! I was so hurt! I was bitter.

I Don't Believe it!

After months of prayer and waiting and allowing the Holy Spirit to work on me, I had gotten past some of that and was trying to believe for miracles and victories to happen! But in that moment, I asked my secretary to call one of the Board members and let him handle it.

Later that day, David, a board member, called me back and said, "Well, Pastor, this man who has the grass, he really does want to give us grass!"

I still didn't believe it. I couldn't believe some stranger out of nowhere would just drive by and want to give me anything. I'm telling you, I was so full of doubt, yet I had been praying FAITH every morning!

Sometimes the miracle God has for us has to knock us down. When it finally happens, you sit there with mouth wide open, incredulous that it really happened. Have you ever had a miracle knock on your door and you just didn't believe it? That's what happened in Acts, Chapter 12. Herod had captured Peter and was determined to execute him.

"Now when Herod was about to bring him out, on that very night, Peter was sleeping between two soldiers, bound with two chains, and sentries before the door were guarding the prison. 7 And behold, an angel of the Lord stood next to him, and a light shone in the cell. He struck Peter on the side and woke him, saying, "Get up quickly." And the chains fell off his hands."
(Acts 12:6-7 ESV)

Who's Knocking?

So Peter goes to John Mark's mother's house, knowing it's safe there. He'll find believers there! In fact, they had been praying he would be released.

"And when he knocked at the door of the gateway, a servant girl named Rhoda came to answer. 14 Recognizing Peter's voice, in her joy she did not open the gate but ran in and reported that Peter was standing at the gate. 15 They said to her, "You are out of your mind." But she kept insisting that it was so, and they kept saying, "It is his angel!" 16 But Peter continued knocking, and when they opened, they saw him and were amazed." (Acts 12:13-16 ESV)

Ok, if you're wondering who Mike Allard is in this story, I'm the guy at the table telling her, "You are out of your mind." Nope, it can't be! That would be a miracle!

Here I was, going to the church every morning, praying and seeking the Lord! Calling on Him to bring us the miracles we needed to get in this building.

Truthfully, I had been believing for this but when the miracle began to happen, I can't say that I was the first to believe it was for real!

So I took the number of the guy with the grass, called him, and told him to meet me at the church property. I thought I would afford him a clearer view of what he didn't see at 55 miles an hour while he was driving by. Yes, it'll be a better picture standing in the weeds and seeing it up close. He'll probably see we don't need grass - we need cash! My thought was that he needs to see how bad it really is. But then again, maybe he's rich and he'll give us m-o-n-e-y so we can finish this m-e-s-s!

Grass?

Really? I'm just being perfectly honest. We didn't need grass! We needed ceiling tiles, paint, wires, and carpet and lights and chairs and we needed mold remediation - you name it, we needed it!

That next morning, a big black truck pulled into the parking lot of the church. A tall, lanky man stepped out of the truck. He had a smile on his face and he shook my hand warmly. He didn't look crazy! He looked legit! He looked normal.

He said, "My name is Steve Roeder, I'm a grass farmer from Crosby, and I was driving by here the other day and the Lord spoke to me and told me to give you all the grass you need!"

I stood there and looked at him like he was speaking Dutch or some other foreign language. I asked him, "What's that going to cost me?" He said, "Well preacher, it's not going to cost you anything, The Lord told me to give you all the grass you need!" Well, I thought to myself that maybe he has bad eyesight and can't see how bad all this looks. I asked him if he wanted to come in and look around. He said, "Yes." So he and I took a tour of the dilapidated interior and I shared our story. I began to tell him how we had bought the land and how the economy had tanked, how we ran out of money, and our finance group had left us high and dry, and how we were in the middle of trying to figure out what to do. He seemed totally unmoved by my words. I had been as negative with a guy as I could without saying why don't you take your grass and plant it somewhere where it will be useful.

Was That a Miracle?

The miracle was standing in the building. It had driven in off the street just as I had prayed it would and I was questioning it. The conflict was real. I just didn't realize how conflicted I was.

He looked at me and said, "Well preacher, the Lord told me driving by here the other day to give you all the grass you need!" As we walked the property, he was trying to be a little more assertive with me. We walked all around the parking lot and we walked all along the retention pond and we walked and walked. He even wrote on a piece of paper like he was measuring stuff. I couldn't believe it. I thought, "He's good! He is good!" I just knew he was going to have some dollar figure at the end that's going to show… "if you let me do this it'll only cost you this amount." You know, like one of those timeshares. They actually make you think you are getting something for free. But, at some point you realize it's not free; there's a gimmick. It's a scam. I had had my share of those and I wasn't going to let this guy pull one over on me. I was older and wiser than when we started this building. I wasn't going to fall for a scam.

Finally we stopped and he said, "Well preacher, I think it's probably going to take about 18, yeah, eighteen-wheelers of grass to do the job!" I looked at him again and said, "So how much is that gonna cost me?" Looking a little frustrated, he paused and looked right at me and said, "Preacher, the Lord told me to give you all the grass you need! No charge!" I told him, "Well, as you can see we're not at the place of needing grass but when I get there I sure will call you. I was baffled, and my unspoken answer was no! He got back into his truck and drove off.

Had I just had a miracle? Did God speak to him? Why didn't it feel like eyes had just opened and deaf ears were now hearing. I was truly caught off guard. I had expected a cost to be presented at the end of our conversation. I had expected the gotcha! I had expected the negative, but God had heard my faith. In spite of my negative attitude, God had sent the answer. He had heard my prayers and those who had prayed with me.

We had knocked on the Lord's door for months and had prayed in faith declaring the things that are not as though they are. We had stood in the unfinished and declared it finished. We had framed our world with the Word of God! We had framed it with faith and said,

"Father send it in… let people drive by and be drawn to give to this ministry so that this can be finished!"

Never Doubt

If there is anything I can speak to you about faith it is this. Never doubt. When you least expect the miracle it will happen and you will be blown away! You can declare the impossible possible. That's not some silly selfish name-it-claim-it babble. That is truth. Jesus said,

"…For truly, I say to you, if you have faith like a grain of mustard seed, you will say to this mountain, 'Move from here to there,' and it will move, and nothing will be impossible for you." (Matthew 17:20 ESV)

We had knocked down the doors of heaven with prayer. We had charged the throne of the Father. We had asked and believed and now my Abba, Daddy, Father God, was knocking me down with His answer!

After he drove off, I walked around the church by myself. I looked at the building and the weeds. I looked at all the debris that I had been seeing and thought of what had just happened. Could God have sent this man!? Could the Lord be trying to tell me something? DUH? You think?

How many times has God sent a boat to rescue you and

you questioned whether it was the right one or whether it was adequate or whether it was the right day or night? All the while He was bringing you the answer.

Jesus repeated this message again in Matthew 21... "Truly, I say to you, if you have faith and do not doubt, you will not only do what has been done to the fig tree, but even if you say to this mountain, 'Be taken up and thrown into the sea,' it will happen.
(Matthew 21:21 ESV)

So stop having this conflict in yourself! Speak the Word of God! Declare the Word of God over the disaster, over the bad news, and believe and watch God throw the mountain in the sea! It will happen!

"And He said to them, "Which of you shall have a friend, and go to him at midnight and say to him, 'Friend, lend me three loaves; 6 for a friend of mine has come to me on his journey, and I have nothing to set before him'; 7 and he will answer from within and say, 'Do not trouble me; the door is now shut, and my children are with me in bed; I cannot rise and give to you'? 8 I say to you, though he will not rise and give to him because he is his friend, yet because of his persistence he will rise and give him as many as he needs." (Luke 11:5-8 ESV)

Persistence

I love that… Not because he was a friend…
"YET BECAUSE OF HIS PERSISTENCE!"

You can't stop! You can't give up! The night of fear is thick with darkness. It's full of shadows and full of things that cause you to want to quit, but you can't! There is an amazing future that He has prepared for you! You don't have to take the present reality that the enemy is trying to tell you is yours. Satan is a liar and the father of lies. Be persistent! The Father will rise and give to you! And when He gets up and starts coming your way… you can't imagine all He will do!

So I stood there and thought and thought about the journey. About the man in the black truck. The grass farmer.

A Love Story

That same week, I was preaching from the book of Ruth! It's a love story. The tiny book describes the troublesome time of a young Moabitess woman who falls in love with an Israelite and marries into his family. They met because of a famine that was in the land of Israel. She lives through the loss of her father-in-law, brother-in-law, and her new husband.   With only Ruth, her daughter-in-law Naomi, and another daughter-in-law, they begin the discussion of returning to Israel. The other sister-in-law bails early and leaves Ruth standing in the dust with Naomi, who wants to change her name to Mara meaning "bitter." Ruth makes a powerful declaration, "I'll go with you! Your God will be my God and your people will be my people!"

So they make the journey back to the family hometown of Bethlehem. Everything was lost and nothing remained of the family wealth. The famine had destroyed their future. What the famine didn't take disease and death had stolen and now two broken women make their way back home!

In that culture it would be impossible for two women to survive without some help. Their only hope was to be able to glean what the farmers left in their fields.

When the rich landlord Boaz comes to inspect his field he spots the beautiful Ruth gathering what the gleaners had left. He is so taken by her, he asks, "Who is that?"

I can just picture her, glancing up with a stare at this handsomely dressed man riding upon his white horse… her hair blowing in the wind, with her black eyes momentarily catching a glance at his eyes. I can imagine him smiling at her and her coyly smiling back at him. She goes back to gathering and he keeps glancing back to her as he tells his workmen to be sure and leave some grain for her on purpose, "I don't want her going to anyone else's field but mine!" I think it was love at first sight!

The interesting thing is that the custom of the day allowed Ruth and Naomi to have their property redeemed if a close person of kin would step in and marry one of them. That would allow the property to be redeemed back to its rightful family line. But how would Ruth or much less Naomi get married here? They were merely beggars in the fields! They had nothing. Nothing to offer! Nothing!

However, a great custom was that a girl could go and lay at the feet of a kinsman and in essence propose to the kinsman and ask him to take care of her. Well, the great part of the story is that Boaz was such a person in relationship to Ruth and Naomi. It was a little more complicated than that but to keep the message short and sweet I focused that week on the fact that Ruth and Naomi had nothing and they needed Boaz more than life. If he were to marry Ruth then they could get their inheritance back. They could survive and thrive as Israelites! They would have a future and a hope!

In the story, when Boaz awakens from sleep and finds the beautiful Ruth laying at his feet partially covered with his tunic... he realizes she wants to come under his protection. He gives her a gift. Instead of a diamond ring he takes her shawl and fills it with six measures of barley seed. Grass seed!

So that Sunday, the week that the grass farmer called, I was already preparing this message about Ruth! God has the best timing, but too many times I don't catch on quickly.

I'm Your Boaz

I was driving down Westlake Houston and the Lord began to speak to me, "I'm your Boaz! I'm going to take care of you! I've heard your prayers and I'm going to make sure you make it!" Tears began to run down my cheeks. I thought of the hopeless and helpless Ruth going to the threshing floor and quietly stepping over to where Boaz was sleeping and lying at his feet! How she needed his help! She pulled his tunic over her slightly, hoping not to wake him too soon. She needed his help to survive!

I needed the Lord more than life! Everything I had done had failed. For months I had journeyed to the church morning after morning praying and asking the Lord.

And this strange gift of grass was about to be the grandest gift I had ever received. What did the story say? He gave her six bushels of barley! At that moment driving in the car with tears running down my face and barely able to see where I was going the Lord said, "I'm not giving you six bushels of grass seed, I'm giving you 18 eighteen-wheelers of grass!" The floodgates of worship and tears began to flow harder... I was overwhelmed with joy! It was as if the Lord was saying, "I know you need a bunch of other stuff too but we are going to finish this!"

With this news, I picked up my phone and called a friend and Board member, Duane Cannon, to tell him this powerful revelation. He was just as excited and being a part of our construction company, he said, "You know pastor, the Lord knows we're going to finish this, because the grass is the last thing we do when we move people into a new building!" I started crying again! Listening to the words were so powerful... "the last thing we do when we move people into a new building!" We were going to move into this building! God was showing me and telling me "I'm your Boaz! I've got this! Don't worry! You're going to make it!"

With many other miracles still to happen, we knew we had grass! To this day, I still get up before the sun rises and go to the church and pray and seek the Lord! At the end of our prayer meeting, those who are with me follow me into the coffee shop. We sit where I used to sit in a camp chair by a kerosene heater and pray in that deserted church building. I now sit in the same spot but in a nice comfortable chair and look out through the windows at... *The Grass.* And I remember! Oh how I remember "who" gave us that grass. I remember the journey and the days of hopelessness; the days of depression; the days of desperation. It seemed they would never end. I wanted to quit! I wanted to give up! But I'm so glad I didn't! I remember the grass farmer and the Lord speaking to that tall, lanky Texan. "The Lord told me to give you all the grass you need!"

When the day came to put that grass down and we called Steve Roeder, we were all excited! It was the last thing we did before moving into the church, at the Crossroads! There have been so many miracles and so many powerful moments that we didn't picture. We were just too excited! Trying to find a picture later wasn't easy. We were so excited no one thought of taking a picture! Later, we found only one. But that picture is imprinted on my heart. Truckload after truckload came into our parking lot. Grass sent by my Abba Father just to let me know He hadn't forgotten His son! He knew exactly where I was. And it was a celebration! We had our future back! It was such a joyful day! It was a day of celebration! That grass represented growth! That grass represented a promise! His promises are yes and amen!

When the great, great, great grandson of Boaz, Solomon, built the temple in Jerusalem he built two pillars at the entrance of the temple.

"Then he set up the pillars before the temple, one on the right hand and the other on the left; he called the name of the one on the right hand Jachin, and the name of the one on the left Boaz." (2 Chronicles 3:17 NKJV)

Boaz means Fleetness or fast... Jachin means strengthens or strong! So as the Israelites entered the Temple they would be reminded that the Lord is fast and strong and that He strengthens us! What seems like a long time in the answer getting to where you are is only a moment for the Lord!

I entered in prayer every morning. I was making the ruins of that unfinished building a house of prayer. The Lord, my Boaz, my Jachin, was listening and hearing our prayers, and He heard us! He came to us and brought the answer!

Let Him be your Boaz today! Call on Him! He will answer! He will not disappoint you! Who knows, maybe someone will call you or knock on your door and say, "The Lord told me to give you all... that you need!"

Let those seeds of faith go deep. Plant in the good soil of your heart! Believe and it will happen! Don't pray in faith and live in doubt! Pray in faith and live in faith and watch the impossible happen! Believe and the mountain will be moved! On the other side of this test is a great testimony!

Victor Numquam Usque!

Believe and
Never Give Up!

Chapter 10
He Taught Me About the Impossible

Things are never impossible!

"…Truly, I say to you, if you have faith and do not doubt, you will not only do what has been done to the fig tree, but even if you say to this mountain, 'Be taken up and thrown into the sea,' it will happen.
(Matthew 21:21 ESV)

"…For truly, I say to you, if you have faith like a grain of mustard seed, you will say to this mountain, 'Move from here to there,' and it will move, and nothing will be impossible for you."
(Matthew 17:20 ESV)

Discussion Questions

Have you ever spoken about faith but lived in fear?
What testimony can you share that shows God still does the impossible?

How Has Faith Changed Your Life?

_____

_____

_____

What is Your Impossible List?

Check the impossible need finished when it's done!

1. _____Done_____
2. _____Done_____
3. _____Done_____
4. _____Done_____
5. _____Done_____
6. _____Done_____
7. _____Done_____
8. _____Done_____
9. _____Done_____
10. _____Done_____

"Nothing is Impossible!"

In September 2010, the grass was finally laid.

Victor Numquam Usque!

Before You Leave...

It was April 16, 2013, when we finally began to clean out what would become the sanctuary.

I have been searching, for quite some time, for a picture of that phase of the journey. It was such an emotional time. I didn't take many pictures during that season. Some days I wanted it to all go away and others I would sit and cry, thanking Him for His provision. What you don't see are all the boxes and things that cluttered that future sanctuary. This was on the day we finally cleaned it all out for the work to begin. I didn't remember this picture even being taken but I think someone captured me sitting there praying. Whether it was a candid or a planned photograph, however it was taken, it is a snapshot of a great place during a great time in my life. I did almost quit but the Lord taught me some great things sitting in that chair. I will always be thankful that He drew me to that place, and the great work He began there.

Many people have asked me, "How did it all work out? How did you end up finishing the building?" I love to tell people it was prayer and missions that made the difference. I believe because we honored God, He blessed us and pushed us forward. I've told the church many times, "We weren't supposed to make it, but with the Lord's help, we did!"

Here are a few of the financial miracles that happened. First, we sold a total of four acres, to two different buyers, for a balance of $1,025,000. Note: during our journey, we found that each miracle came with its own impossibilities. One of the buyers made a stipulation that both closings had to happen on the same day or they were out. If you've ever bought property you understand that it's not always easy with closings and financing, maybe even impossible for such a demand to happen, but it did, just as they requested.

The second thing that occurred was we asked our people to "fund" an unsecured bond issue of $750,000. They agreed and a half-dozen or so of our faithful saints put up their life savings and we borrowed their money, at 6% interest – interest only, for three years. At the time, we weren't sure when or how we would pay their money back, but they were all in! It actually turned out that after three years we gave all of them a 10% bonus to let us continue the loans. The Bible calls that a Selah Moment. Simply put, "Think on that!"

Just about the time you worry how will this all work out, God always has a way. And His way is usually shocking and unexpected. We had prayed and prayed and finally we were able to occupy the building with just 300 people. Like Gideon's army of 300, we possessed the land, and it was amazing!

I'll never forget that day. It was a Wednesday. September 5, 2010, that we finally occupied the new church at 12110 East Sam Houston Parkway North. We were so excited! We threw together an impromptu service that night, and had a wonderful time of worship and praise. A portable sound system was set up in the commons. Thankfully we had some folding chairs and around 50-60 people gathered for church. I preached, and we thanked the Lord for His goodness. For years now, the first Sunday of September has become "sweet Sunday!" It's a day we remember how sweet the Lord has been to us, and we always eat sweets that day!

Back when we finally moved into the church, we didn't have the funds to complete the main auditorium so we remodeled the fellowship hall into a chapel. It would hold around 300 people, but we still needed to finish the 700-seat main sanctuary.

For three years the Lord helped us to grow. By the time we were 800 people, we received an incredible miracle surprise!

Time and time again, I had prayed and told the Lord, "Now would be a good time for a miracle!" It never came until we had outgrown the chapel and had to get into the main sanctuary.

Unexpectedly an inheritance from a precious 97-year-old man who attended our church, was given to us. His son who had died had left his father his full retirement. When all was finally received, the church was blessed with over $1.5 million. Finally, we completed the main auditorium. It had been five years since we poured the foundation. But it was ten years from the time we had bought the property and finished that phase. Ten years is a long time, but in a building program, in pastor years, it feels like a lifetime!

Overall we have been blessed! We've watched the hand of the Lord again and again stretch out over us and provide in supernatural ways. We have spoken things that are not as though they are and God has blessed us again and again.

Today, Crossroads Fellowship has more than 1,500 weekend attenders, with several thousand calling it home.

One of our core values has been the Great Commission! With missions as a priority with the Lord's help, we have been able to give over $1 million for missions, each year since 2017.

In April of 2016, we started a new extension campus, and in February of 2017, we began another new church in the inner city of downtown Houston.

I challenge you if you've wanted to give up and wondered how it would all work out. Remember, we had no hope of a turnaround. There was no possible way that it would ever work out. As we prayed and believed God – HE pushed us forward into a greater destiny. It was messy. It was hard. It was the most trying time of my ministry. But it made me and this church into what it is today – a vibrant, loving community of believers, who will…

NEVER GIVE UP!

In Closing...

To my wife, Danielle, how could I have made it through all the difficult days without you? Thank you for being my companion on this great journey and most of all, my best friend. I love you more than you will ever know. Thank you for not letting me quit! Without the Lord Jesus and you, I never would have made it.

To Del, Brad and Sharon, those early faithful partners in prayer. Your faithfulness to God's house to pray kept me going. When I wanted to quit I was reminded of those who held my hands up. You stayed when others fled; you walked with me when others doubted; you believed when others shook in fear; you've been the greatest blessing. Thank you!

To the many who have walked with me since. The faithful who still pray with me each morning and help carry the burden of this amazing ministry. You are my dearest friends and companions.

To Joshua, Michael, Lacey, Melissa, Alicia and RC. A father couldn't ask for better children. Thank you for loving me even when I was unlovable during my dark days. I love you!

To my father and mother in love, thank you for your love

and support and the many hours you prayed for me. Thank you for your constant love and guidance in the tough times of my life.

To my amazing staff and board, thank you for being what I needed. I'm so glad I didn't make this journey alone. You were there and felt much of the same pain and agony. Your love and faithfulness has touched my life. I will forever be grateful to the support you have given me.

To friends like Dr. Alon Barak and his wife Ronit, who encouraged me to complete this work and get it into print. Thank you for your help and the love and support you have given.

To Kenneth Hall and your incredible edits and insights into the writing of this book. What a timely meeting in a moment of need. Thank you.

To the many saints at Crossroads, thank you for loving this pastor during my greatest trial. You have encouraged me; prayed for me; lifted me; blessed me; held me; and given so much to me.

I love you!
Mike

You can access this book through **Kindle** Unlimited or pay $7.99 to buy on Kindle.

Paperback copies $9.99 through

Never Give Up!
Lessons the Lord Taught Me When I Wanted to Quit!

For Testimonials
...of how you have been affected by the book Never Give Up and its effect on your life please send an email directly to Pastor Mike at: mikeallard@mac.com

Crossroads Fellowship
713-455-1661
12110 E Sam Houston Pkwy N
Houston, Texas 77044

Another Book by Mike Allard

You can access this book through the **Amazon** Bookstore or purchase on campus at Crossroads Fellowship.

Paperback copies $14.99 through Amazon.com

Walk with Pastor Mike Allard as he takes us on a journey listening to true stories of people who have decided to live in the overflow of Christ's life. These stories will cause you to laugh, cry, and inspire you to join them in the joy of generosity. You will find insights into his life and great encouragement for yours within the pages of this book. He reveals other truths about how you can experience life to the fullest. How having a daily time in prayer and allowing the Holy Spirit to flow through you will move you into the overflow. He holds nothing back about what the Bible says about a Spirit-empowered life! You will experience a deeper understanding of ministry and the blessing of serving others. And just as he did in the book Never Give Up, you'll hear about his own failures, and his own need for a deeper walk with Christ. He reveals insights into some of his own weaknesses in leading. We all need rest. We all need a time of refreshing. We all need to resist the temptation to only think of ourselves. Every chapter will have a surprise and will cause you to move from the ordinary to the extraordinary. Living in the Overflow is about being generous in every area of your life. It's serving like Christ. It's moving forward in His Great Commission. Once we take the focus off of ourselves, we can truly experience that overflow!

Large Orders of "<u>Never Give Up!</u>" or "<u>Living in the Overflow!</u>"

Special Pricing is available for quantities over 25 copies. Please feel free to contact Pastor Mike through the above email!

About the Author

Reverend Mike Allard began preaching as a boy when he was just thirteen years old in his home church, Northwest Assembly of God in Wichita Falls, Texas. He received his first preaching credential, The Christian Worker's Permit, March 9, 1976, at the age of fifteen. He was licensed at nineteen and has been ordained for the past thirty-three years.

During his years of ministry, he has served as youth pastor and children's pastor for eleven years; as District Youth Director in South Texas for eleven years and the Lead Pastor at Crossroads Fellowship, in Houston, Texas for the past eighteen years.

He was elected to the South Texas District Assemblies of God Presbytery as an Executive Presbyter in 2016.

He is the author of the book: "Never Give Up!" It is the incredible true story of how God brought him from failure to faith.

Crossroads Fellowship, under the leadership of Pastor Mike has grown from 250 to an average of 1,500 each Sunday.

Pastor Mike has a passion for souls and missions. In his many years of travel, he has raised millions of dollars in mission services, conferences, conventions, camps, tours, and on special days. Over the past three years, Crossroads Fellowship has given each year over $1,000,000 to missions.

But his greatest accomplishment is his family. He has a beautiful wife Danielle who has been by his side for 40 years. He has three wonderful children, Joshua, Michael and Lacey. He has ten grandchildren, and he looks forward to every day getting to share life with this crazy, wonderful family God has given him.

Victor Numquam Usque!

Made in the USA
Columbia, SC
23 April 2022

59373086R00124